Christians in the Culture

Pursuing Jesus in the 21st Century Western World

Matthew Allen, Mitch Stevens, Keith Stonehart, Ken Weliever,
Clay Gentry, Todd Chandler, Roger Shouse, Max Dawson, Reuben Prevost,
Buddy Payne, Art Adams, Shane Scott, Andrew Roberts, and Don Truex

Edited by Matthew Allen

Published by
Spiritbuilding Publishers
9700 Ferry Road, Waynesville, OH 45068

CHRISTIANS IN THE CULTURE:
Pursuing Jesus in the 21st Century Western World
Matthew Allen, Mitch Stevens, Keith Stonehart, Ken Weliever, Clay Gentry, Todd Chandler, Roger Shouse, Max Dawson, Reuben Prevost, Buddy Payne, Art Adams, Shane Scott, Andrew Roberts, and Don Truex
Edited by Matthew Allen

ISBN: 978-1-955285-06-3

Spiritbuilding
PUBLISHERS

spiritbuilding.com
Spiritual Equipment for the Contest of Life

Table of Contents

Foreword 2

Lecture 1 Engaging Modern Culture 4
Matthew Allen

Lecture 2 Raising a Christian Family in a Secular Culture 21
Mitch Stevens

Lecture 3 Representing Jesus on Social Media 34
Keith Stonehart

Lecture 4 The Role of the Church in Society 43
Ken Weliever

Lecture 5 Love and Sex 54
Clay Gentry

Lecture 6 A Christian and Transgenderism 62
Todd Chandler

Lecture 7 The Christian and Politics 77
Roger Shouse

Lecture 8 Christians and Race 83
Max Dawson and *Reuben Prevost*

Lecture 9 Can Christianity and Science Coincide? 92
Dr. H.E. "Buddy" Payne, Jr.

Lecture 10 The Church: A Place of Healing 107
Art Adams

Lecture 11 Christians and Higher Education 116
Shane Scott

Lecture 12 Interacting with Other Faiths 126
Andrew Roberts

Lecture 13 Judges or Messengers? 136
Don Truex

The lessons you are about to read in this book were presented at the Cornerstone Church of Christ in Centerville, Ohio, over the summer of 2021. Videos and presentation files of each can be found at cornerstone-coc.com.

Cornerstone Church of Christ, formerly known as Kettering Church of Christ, is a family of believers in the Dayton, Ohio area. Comprised of over 90 families who live all over southwestern Ohio, the growing congregation is committed to glorifying Jesus in His kingdom through reverent worship; a continuing commitment to local and foreign outreach; and internal spiritual upbuilding and development. The congregation is served by three shepherds, Rich Walker, George Wacks, and Russ Robins. Matthew Allen and Cain Atkinson serve as ministers.

We heartily commend each of the lessons you are about to read and hope you will find them to be not only informative and relevant to our day, but also uplifting and encouraging.

Be blameless and pure, children of God who are faultless in a crooked and perverted generation, among whom you shine like stars in the world (Philippians 2:15).

cornerstone-coc.com

Foreword

For us, living in this world could be likened to being a fish swimming in a river against the current. Every decision we make plays a role in the direction we swim. It is always easier to go with the current—the way of least resistance. For some fish however, going downstream leads them straight into the jaws of a predator.

For a long time, Christians have not had to do much "swimming against the current." Generations before benefited from the Judeo-Christian worldview that dominated western culture. Now, the sun appears to be setting on those days. We do not need to panic or react in unadulterated anger toward this reality. We should understand it, accept it and learn how to swim God's way no matter how strong the current against us becomes.

An entirely new framework and value system not built on Christian principles has taken root throughout our nation and the western world at large. Many of these implications, values, societal doctrines and creeds come from a stream of thought flowing down from the basin of secular humanism. The current is strong, and it is pulling many people away from the true stream that leads to the river of life.

> Do not believe every spirit, but test the spirits to see if they are from God (1 John 4:1).

Christians have the responsibility to address these current issues. But this must be done objectively and carefully. As ambassadors of Christ, we must engage people in a way that allows us to minister to a sin-sick world. It should not be our aim to debate an invisible opponent, preach politics, rehearse long-held beliefs, or to "show how righteous we are." Rather, our job is to provide grace, humility, and transparency in love to all who hear. We hope this book can be used as a productive tool for others in leading the type of conversations that bring the kingdom increase, and ultimately, bring glory to Christ.

> You are the salt of the earth, but if salt has lost its taste, how shall its saltiness be restored? It is no longer good for anything except to be thrown out and trampled under people's feet. You are the light of the world. A city set on a hill cannot be hidden. Nor do people light a lamp and put it under a basket, but on a stand, and it gives light to all in the house. In the same way, let your light shine before others, so that they may see your good works and give glory to your Father who is in heaven (Matthew 5:13–16).

Christianity is inherently a counter-cultural movement. It is not a political movement that bends to the right or to the left. Rather, it transcends every human system by its being designed to bring people together around the cross of Christ. It has the power to bring all people to experience the depth of God's goodness in whatever culture they live. Christians have been imperfectly seeking to achieve this goal since the first century. It is our prayer that no matter what perspective you are coming from, that the text in this book will offer a perspective that is based in God's character, as being eternally just and righteous, as well as eternally loving and merciful. We pray for open minds and humility on all sides of the conversation, and we pray you, the reader, are blessed.

Lecture 1

Engaging Modern Culture

Matthew Allen

A Look Back

I came of age during the 1980s and early 90s, growing up in a small town in southwest Arkansas, a little less than halfway between Little Rock and Texarkana. Affectionately known as the *Brick Capital of the World,* Malvern was, and still is, a close-knit community. What I remember about it is mostly good. Looking back, if a person didn't know you, they most certainly knew who your parents or grandparents were ... or they would know someone in your extended family or church family. Just about everyone was connected in some way. It was common to walk into the *Food Center,* where my uncle still works, and see people from all over the community stopped in the aisles asking about friends and family ... catching up on life. We knew just about everyone on our street. Clint Fuller, who lived on the corner, was a referee for the Southwest Conference who sometimes got to work some of the Razorback games when they would play in Little Rock. Mrs. Frances Rutherford and Mrs. Merle Hardin, both widowed, lived next door to us with our little house in between. They each knew my grandmother from her earlier life when her first husband was a deacon at First Baptist Church. Merle's husband, Ed, worked with my grandfather in the post office after WW2. Across the street was Mr. Fred Giles and the Collins family lived next door to him. Guy Collins worked for a HVAC company and his wife, Sheila, attended pharmacy school in Little Rock. Their son, George and I played together all the time. Around the corner was the neighborhood grocery store, Mitchell's. Mitchell Burris had owned the store for years and his two sons, Mike and Mark, were in the process of taking over the business. They both went to school with my mom and were leading members in the Pentecostal church where my future wife grew up.

I remember how most families spent their entire life in Hot Spring County and people moving in were a big deal. With those who left, we never could figure out why anyone would want to ever move away. It was a big deal for us to go to Little Rock for a shopping trip. *If you had been up there, you had been somewhere.* Our community was safe. Mom and Dad never minded me riding my bicycle all over town on those hot, humid summer days. Fishing with friends, floating on the river, being out in the woods with your 410 or 22, was just a part of regular life. Our high school parking lot was filled mainly with trucks ... most of them with gun racks in the back window ... with shot guns and rifles ready for hunting. *No one thought anything about it.* Some of the rural schools in our county cancelled school during the first week of November when deer season began. They knew hunting was a family affair.

There was a basic trust and expectation among people to do the right thing ... work hard, be honest, and treat people right. Most people were religious. On Sunday morning as we drove to church, every parking lot of every local church was full. I remember the uproar in town when the big retailer Wal-Mart decided to open from 12–5 on Sunday afternoons. Our elderly Southern Baptist neighbors resolved they would never shop in any store that was open on the *Christian Sabbath.* Like many counties in Arkansas, Hot Spring County was a dry county with no alcohol sales allowed. No school district in our county would have ever decided to schedule a sporting or extracurricular event on a Wednesday night or a Sunday. Those times were reserved for church. There was a basic Christian morality that permeated everything we did. Even though there were big doctrinal disagreements between us, Christian influence was strong everywhere you went.

Looking back, my world revolved around that area and that culture ... and I loved it. And maybe, as you've read my trip down memory lane you can feel the nostalgia. When I'm back for a visit, there are things about it that I miss. Other things, not so much. And while I've painted a mostly positive picture (I think all of us do as we reflect on culture decades in the past), it must not be misunderstood that I think everything was perfect. There were dishonest people. Immorality was rampant. Liquor stores abounded at the county line. All of that was in the background. If you looked for it, you would have seen broken marriages; abused kids; and racism rearing its ugly head. The court system had plenty of work. People went to jail. Churches had their scandals and squabbles. It would not be fair to pretend those things did not exist.

Today's World is Much Different

But the way of life I remember growing up seems, in many ways, so much simpler and innocent now, especially as we consider our present world. I'm writing just days after mass shootings in the Atlanta and Denver suburbs. The media is desperately looking for someone or an ideology to blame. Two weeks ago, a major music awards show featured an act that was little more than soft pornography danced to a "song" with explicit lyrics. The broadcast was rated TV-14 and did not include any warning about the nature of the performance beforehand. Pop culture raved about it. Last week a transgendered man became the first person of that lifestyle to become a Senate-confirmed government official. It was applauded across the Washington punditry as a major step forward in the battle of equality for transexuals. This week a columnist for USA Today has called for Oral Roberts University's basketball team to be booted from the NCAA basketball tournament because the schools "deeply bigoted anti-LGBTQ+ policies can't and shouldn't be ignored."[1] And finally, this past Monday the U.S. Court of Appeals denied an appeal of a Washington football coach who was fired after his seven-year practice of praying with players at the 50-yard line at the conclusion of each high school football game. It was said that some players felt they were not in an inclusive and welcoming environment as they prayed.

Looking across the landscape, many of us see a world that is hard to recognize as we remember the unique experiences of our past American culture. So many things have changed. How much farther can we go as these things not only continue, but grow more prevalent? What will happen when we are told to not only be silent on speaking out against immorality, but instead to actively affirm and celebrate it? Why is the topic of Christian persecution inside the United States even entertained as a growing possibility in the not too far distant future? Why are our children growing up thinking the country will dissolve into a bitter civil war over the next few years?

---

1 Jhaveri, Hemal. "Oral Roberts University Isn't the Feel Good March Madness Story We Need." Retrieved 03/25/21 from https://ftw.usatoday.com/2021/03/oral-roberts-ncaa-anti-lgbtq-code-of-conduct.

It is not the same world many of us grew up in. We're more educated and wealthier. Our access to information is instantaneous. As a result, we're more impatient. We are the center of our own universe. We're arrogant, thinking we know more than we do. We get around more than we used to, decreasing the level of connectedness we used to take for granted. For example, families have become more transient, often living hundreds or even thousands of miles away from where they were raised. Most have brought their own culture, language, and value system along, which may look very different from our own.[2] Here in the Midwest, while most people in our communities may identify as religious, now Christianity is only one of many religious varieties from which to choose. And while religious identity may still be the norm, it certainly feels like those who identify as Christian are part of a growing minority, especially if you intend to live out the principles and be faithful in attending worship.[3] While this is certainly not the first time in world history Christians have ever found themselves in a minority, it is the first time in this country's existence that there is an active resistance to and wholesale rejection of Christianity by American society at large. Many of the values we took for granted just a few short decades ago are now being lost to the passage of time.

Today it is normal for our children to go off to school and be confronted with immorality on a scale we could have never imagined when we were children. Each day our young people are being trained to question authority and the Biblical virtues we have raised them on. They are told their parents have subscribed to antiquated and fundamentalist views. And not only that, they are also shamed into thinking that those who espouse traditional Judeo-Christian morality are the ones with dark hearts, who are nothing more than racist bigots and nationalists who are just mad that their time of domination, "privilege," and exclusivism has passed.

2 The wife of a preaching friend of mine who lives outside of Seattle reports that there are over 140 languages represented in the school system she works for.

3 A Gallup Survey from March 29, 2021 reveals church membership inside the United States is now less than 50%. See "U.S. Church Membership Falls Below Majority for First Time." https://news.gallup.com/poll/341963/church-membership-falls-below-majority-first-time.aspx?.

At younger and younger ages, they are being bombarded with sex ... and the other side seems intent on acquainting them with every possible form of deviance ... all in the name of tolerance and open-mindedness. Anyone who would dare question these new cultural crusaders must be silenced at all costs. Our institutions of higher learning have become a moral cesspool where godliness is resisted not only among the student body, but the new, *enlightened, and informed* secular-humanist system is championed by administrators and faculty alike. Any diversion from the agenda must not only be silenced, but it also must be *punished and destroyed.* As we observe our world, the appearance is that young minds are being not only swayed ... but fundamentally and permanently changed.

Impact on the Church

The impact is spilling over into the church. Today, a typical congregation in the church of Christ will lose half its young people to the world once they leave home. Flavil Yeakley[1]—who almost a decade ago in his studies of growth patterns within the churches of Christ—found that around 42% of our young people are leaving the church. In my own experience, working with two Midwestern suburban congregations over the last 18 years, the number of young people who have left hovers between 50–60%. Kids now, on a daily basis, confront matters Gen X'ers and Boomers once took for granted. At younger and younger ages, they're facing matters on the existence of God, the validity and authority of Scripture, sexual morality, gender issues, legalization of drugs, cohabitation, and many other things. Many local church curriculum programs fail in addressing these matters in a modern/relevant way. Some have dismissed these concerns by refusing to budge in their teaching methods, using the same teaching style of the 1950's and 60's. Kids simply do not learn this way anymore. Others operate with dismissive tones and sweeping generalizations regarding our young people all in direct earshot. Still others take it for granted that our young people know how much we love and care for them. They may hear words, but actions are lacking. And yes, while some of the criticisms of young people

1 Yeakley, Flavil. *Why They Left: Listening to Those Who Have Left Churches of Christ.* Nashville: Gospel Advocate, 2012, p. 39. Yeakley says that around 21% leave for denominational groups and another 21% leave their faith behind altogether.

today are valid, the bulk of the responsibility lies on their adult parents and influencers who have refused first, to become aware of the type and breadth of problems young people today face, or second, become so wrapped up in their lives that their kids have had to teach themselves about morality and religion through YouTube or TikTok.

Sadly, as they've come of age, our young people are leaving the church and not coming back. Some of our congregations now have mostly empty classrooms and little hope of younger families moving in to change the dynamic and turn the growth trajectory around. As the remaining members sit there, Sunday after Sunday, turning grayer while they stare at empty pews and classrooms, it is easy to become jaded and maybe just a little embittered. Instead of looking with introspection, externalizing the problem requires much less effort. And that is what happens. Everything becomes "us vs. them," "we are right, everyone else is wrong," or "why can't they just see and accept the truth?" "They don't love the truth as much as we do and want something soft and more lenient." "They aren't interested in working in a church ... they just want to hide in the background in a larger church." The statements could just go on and on. A generation down the road when these congregations close their doors forever, some will only then begin to ask in dismay, *How did this happen? How did we get here?*

What Can We Do Now? How Do We Respond?

Many more paragraphs could be written as we try to properly frame the problem we face. (It is so wide and encompassing that I'm not sure I've done it justice in the paragraphs you've just read.) The hearts of most are pure. The last thing they want is for their congregation to die or those they love to drift away from God. But a new reality has come upon us, which may be hard to accept. This is no longer a culture where Christian influence is in the majority. I take no pleasure in saying this. As we come to grips with this, we may feel shell-shocked as the hits keep coming with increasing rapidity. In these moments we may not be certain on how to respond. In fact, many of us are probably somewhere along a progression as we access the cultural landscape ... dealing with all sorts of emotions ... much like the key points of what is referred to as the *five stages of grief.*

In her 1969 book *On Death and Dying,* Elisabeth Kübler-Ross outlined a basic five-step progression[1] on how people cope with terminal illness and dying. Her book has sold millions and been printed in over 40 different languages. Over the last 50 years the model she outlined has been adapted to apply to almost any dramatic life changing situation. In a 2014 book published after her death and co-authored by David Kessler, Kübler-Ross writes that the five stages of grief can happen after any form of personal loss.[2] In other studies, some academics now identify this as *The Change Curve.* [3]They describe it in three stages, with the second stage being the lowest emotional point.

As you cope with the changing moral standards and rejection of Christianity, you may go through periods of:

- **Shock and Denial.** Some of the things we see, read, and hear about are shocking. We don't know how to respond. So, we cope by holding onto a reality that no longer exists. Our thoughts drift to the past. Mentally and emotionally, we reject the clear and obvious truth before us. We ignore the problem by turning off the news, getting away from social media, or avoid other ways of "being in the know" as to what is happening with the culture. Others try to convince themselves that change isn't going to happen, or if it does, it won't affect them. They try to carry on as they always have and may deny they know about the changes and avoid planning in how to deal with those changes.
- **Anger and Depression.** This is where we decide to fight back against the fear. We're still living in denial, thinking that we have power to change the problem. So, we begin to blame others or an ideology. We reinforce our stereotypes and lash out at all who may be different or younger than us. I believe this is why our social media feeds are so

1 The Five-Step Process outlined by Kübler-Ross is: 1) Denial; 2) Anger; 3) Bargaining; 4) Depression; and 5) Acceptance.

2 Examples might be the loss of a job or decrease in income; major rejection; the end of a relationship or divorce; drug addiction; incarceration; the onset of disease; or even minor losses such as the loss of insurance coverage. See Kübler-Ross, E., Kessler D. *On Grief and Grieving: Finding the Meaning of Grief Through Five Stages of Loss.* New York. Scribner, 2014.

3 the_change_curve.pdf (exeter.ac.uk)

negative. Christians have become adept at expressing their frustration, irritation, and anxiety through the outlet of social media as they cope with political and social change. It is seen in our suspicion, skepticism, and frustration. While most of the time we keep this hidden behind a keyboard, sometimes it comes out through rude behavior or ... worse. This is all before we reach the lowest part of the emotional curve, where depression sets in. Now, reality is beginning to be acknowledged. This often leads to feelings of being overwhelmed which morph into apathy and isolation. Our self-talk may sound like this: *What's the point? Why even try? It's never going to get better.* The situation appears to be locked in with no possibility of change. Things are hopeless. There is the thought of flight. How many people have you heard speak of their desire to move to a different part of the country that aligns closer to their values ... or even move to another country? These are real conversations people are having.

- **Acceptance and Integration.** This is the final stage where a person comes to terms with the reality of the situation, i.e., we've lost the culture war and that's okay. And it's okay because, as Brian Mesimer writes, "the Christian hopes not in solely the political process but in the active working of God."[4] It's not easy to get this final part of the process, but as we do, our emotions will improve and we will learn to work inside the change instead of against it. Christians and local congregations will look for new opportunities and move in faith, hope, and trust.

Defining and Living inside Culture

What do we mean when we use the word *culture?* Sometimes we use it to refer to what we might call *high culture,* i.e., the arts, music, sculpture, paintings, etc. At other times, we might be referencing *pop culture,* i.e., TV shows, movies, Hollywood, or music. And finally, there may be times we use it to describe anything that is against what we believe as a Christian. We tend to only use the word when we're referring to ungodly music, immoral lifestyles, liberal politics, social agendas, movies, and immodest dress, just to name a few. Generally, we use the word to refer to worldliness.

4 Mesimer, Brian. "The Five Stages of Evangelical Grief." Mereorthodoxy.com. Retrieved 03/26/2021 from *The Five Stages of Evangelical Grief | Mere Orthodoxy.*

Two Definitions

In its most basic sense, *culture is what people do with the world.*[1] This includes good things and bad, things morally neutral and morally complex. Stonestreet and Kunkle explain that people make culture and are shaped by culture, but it would be wrong to equate them with culture. Culture is what people do as a people.

Bruce Ashford's definition is similar. Culture is:

> Anything humans produce when they interact with each other and God's creation. People produce food, build things, develop worldviews, and practice religion. Humans produce culture and simultaneously allow it to shape them, affecting who they are, what they think, and how they feel.[2]

Broadly speaking, culture encompasses the totality of life in this world. It is constantly changing. It is never in a fixed position. Some of us have been around long enough to see things come into style, go out of style, and come back into style. The way we use language is also an example. Yesterday, our second preacher walked in the office and complimented me using a word that twenty years ago I associated with an insult. What was out then is cool and hip now. Culture is dynamic. "Culture changes according to human innovations, inventions, fashions and ideas. What one generation considers normal, the next generation thinks of as odd or funny. In the same way, grandparents shake their heads at the fashions, entertainment choices, values, and lifestyles of the young, and vice versa."[3]

Cultures are perpetuated through ideas. These are often generated by artists (songs and books, etc.), storytellers (books, TV shows, movies, documentaries, etc.), entrepreneurs (and their marketers), and educators. These ideas are then maintained and circulated by institutions. Our system

---

1 Stonestreet, John & Kunkle, Brett. *A Practical Guide to Culture: Helping the Next Generation Navigate Today's World.* Colorado Springs, CO: David C. Cook.

2 Ashford, Bruce Riley. *Every Square Inch: An Introduction to Cultural Engagement for Christians.* Bellingham, WA: Lexham Press, 2015, p. 13.

3 Stonestreet & Kunkle.

of higher education is an example. Government is another. Media, family, and the church would be more examples. As you think of these institutions, over the course of your lifetime, which have become of lesser influence? Which have become more? As Satan has worked through educators, media, and government, family and church have declined in the way they impact society. "As the church becomes less important in the everyday lives of citizens, other sources of moral authority become more important, for better or worse."[4]

So how does the Christian relate to culture? It is essential to get this right. If we do not, it will be detrimental not only to our life, but to the world around us. If we get it right, it will transform our lives and the lives of those around us.

Two Perspectives

Christians Against Culture

In his book, Ashford describes this as looking at the church like a bomb shelter.[5] It's very easy to do in our post-Christian world, especially as our theological and moral values are being rejected and mocked in the public square. So, in this viewpoint, the idea is to protect or even withdraw from the culture at large. And, taking in the three levels of *The Change Curve* mentioned previously, it could be very easy to sequester ourselves.

There are good motives and intentions behind it. There are Biblical principles here as well. Christians have been called upon to be pure and holy, as well as to protect themselves from ungodly influences:

- Hebrews 12:14[6]: *Pursue peace with everyone, and holiness—without it no one will see the Lord.*
- 2 Corinthians 7:1b: *Let us cleanse ourselves from every impurity of the flesh and spirit, bringing holiness to completion in the fear of God.*

---

4 *Ibid.*

5 Ashford, p. 12.

6 All my scripture references are taken from the *Christian Standard Bible.*

- 1 Peter 1:14–16: *As obedient children, do not be conformed to the desires of your former ignorance. But as the one who called you is holy, you also are to be holy in all your conduct; for it is written, Be holy, because I am holy.*
- 1 Peter 2:11: *Dear friends, I urge you as strangers and exiles to abstain from sinful desires that wage war against the soul.*

It is very true that the church is a place of refuge and protection and a place where we can be spiritually healed, renewed, and refreshed. But the battle is not in our buildings, it's out in the world. We must never retreat behind our four walls and sit down and wait for the world to end. The battle rages outside and we need to see ourselves as vessels transmitting the power that can change hearts and minds.

It was Jesus who said:

> I have given them your word. The world hated them because they are not of the world, just as I am not of the world. I am not praying that you take them out of the world but that you protect them from the evil one. They are not of the world, just as I am not of the world (John 17:14–16)

As you read this verse, did you discover the two takeaways? We are in the world, but not of it. Isolation is not an option. We can't remove ourselves from this world.

Christianity is not only about militant resistance. When we frame Christianity as being against culture, we view everything primarily from the perspective of warfare. And yes, we are at war:

- Ephesians 6:11 instructs us to put on the whole armor of God.
- 1 Timothy 6:12 tells us to fight the good fight of faith.
- James 4:7 contains an imperative to resist the devil.
- 2 Corinthians 10:4–5 urges us to cast down philosophies that are against God.

Spiritual warfare is not the totality of our existence. We must remember as we look out across the culture that it is full of lost *people* in need of rescue.

Christians help people. Like Jesus, we have a heart for the lost (Mark 2:17). We have been called to exhibit the love of God (John 13:34–35).

Christianity In and For the Culture

Going back to our passage in John 17:14–16, Christianity *in* and *for* the culture is the essence of these verses. We don't withdraw from the culture, leading lives of isolation and fear, we engage with it where we can, viewing ourselves as representatives of Christ who live for the good of others. We accomplish this by consistent obedience that glorifies Jesus and by providing effective testimony for the gospel.

It is very easy to see how the world is running off the proverbial cliff ... away from God as fast as possible. All around we see people worshipping themselves, sex, money, power, or *anything* other than God. It is our job to speak out against these things *from the perspective of pointing the way to help.* This is what we mean by living *for* the culture. We're speaking out for their sake. We point the way to healing. We are there to help. We show people how to redirect their lives. *We bring solutions, not condemnation and judgment.* This is the spirit behind Jesus' instruction in Matthew 5:13–16. Notice how we are:

- Salt, preserving all that is good, right, and wholesome (Matthew 5:13).
- Light, acting in a way to bring God glory in all we do (Matthew 5:14). Whether it be how we engage others in social media, on the job, in the public square, wherever.

Our Directive for Responding to Culture

> Therefore, if anyone is in Christ, he is a new creation; the old has passed away, and see, the new has come! Everything is from God, who has reconciled us to himself through Christ and has given us the ministry of reconciliation. That is, in Christ, God was reconciling the world to himself, not counting their trespasses against them, and he has committed the message of reconciliation to us. Therefore, we are ambassadors for Christ, since God is making his appeal through us. We plead on Christ's behalf, "Be reconciled to God." He made the

> one who did not know sin to be sin for us, so that in him we might become the righteousness of God (2 Corinthians 5:17–21).

As we examine this passage, we find a directive for how to live while we live in this world, as we wait on the world to come. Paul instructs Christians to go forward with a ministry of reconciliation—first with an understanding of their new identity, i.e., *they are a new creation.* This is a present reality for every baptized believer. You live in this reality. Your newness results from your being *in Christ.*

In vv. 18–19 we learn three things:

1. God wants to reconcile sinners to Himself through Christ.
2. Upon that reconciliation, we each have been given *the ministry of reconciliation.* Our focus is outward, toward the lost. It is service based.
3. We have been given a *message.* The word for "message" is *logos* in the original language, which in this case is referencing the gospel. The gospel *message* is that *God was reconciling the world to himself, not counting their trespasses against them.* Every Christian has been entrusted with the purpose to get that message out to as many as possible.

The Imagery of an Ambassador

Notice 2 Corinthians 5:20. Since God is making His appeal through us, we are *ambassadors for Christ.* An ambassador is a position of dignity and honor whereby a person represents the government in a foreign land. When we travel overseas, we are subjected to different traditions and lifestyles, many of which will run counter to our own. My travels to Colombia have taken me to Manizales during the time of the running of the bulls. It's a festive time filled with a party atmosphere. Lewd women, abundant alcohol, and the absence of restraint abound. When I've been in the country during that time, those are events I don't participate in. Getting gored is not my thing, plus it's important to keep myself away from temptation and sin. But at the same time, while I am there, I am on a mission. Bull fighting is not my mission. Representing Jesus Christ is.

The apostles often stressed that we are citizens of heaven dwelling in a foreign land. This world is not our home. But while we are here, we proclaim the message of reconciliation as an ambassador representing the eternal King. It is not our own personal dignity that brings power and influence to our role, it is that of the One we represent. It is not our own message, words, or demands that carry weight ... it is the words we have been given to speak by Jesus through His revealed word. As we speak, we need to remember it is not our job to change the culture, our job is simply to represent the One who sent us.

We Need to Stay on Track

For the last forty years, American evangelicals have been locked in moral, political, and cultural battles. The *Moral Majority* has largely failed in its mission to accomplish lasting and sweeping cultural change through the usage of politics. In fact, most politicians have used and manipulated many God-fearing and noble Christians who were moving with the best of intentions, to accomplish their own ends. Most politicians have no genuine desire to enact laws that encourage moral living. How many years have we been promised real and lasting change on abortion laws? Time after time, when Congress has had the ability, the politicians have found a way not to act. And think about the number of corrupt "Christian" leaders who have held influential positions inside the *Moral Majority* over our lifetime. Every time, those in the media and society have heaped scorn upon evangelicals and unfairly branded us all as being either hypocrites or dumb and naïve sheep. Organizations like *Focus on the Family* have used the courts to fight and protect our children from the cultural left. Little, if any ground has been gained. The tide of cultural rot and decay only seems to grow by the day... as those opposed to Christ grow in their intensity and determination. When it comes effecting national repentance and change, evangelicals have been stymied. It's only led to more frustration as we've moved off track.

And without realization, this has led to some viewing those in the mission field as the enemy. Please reread 2 Corinthians 5:19–20. Our directive is to circulate and promote *the message;* not fix the culture. Our mission is the gospel, not politics. Our aim is to change *individual* lives because changed lives impacted by the gospel is what will change society. God's mission has never deviated. We see it in the mission of Jonah, who saw the Ninevites as nothing more than wretched and depraved enemies who hated all that was good. He had ample evidence upon which to build his case. The Assyrian nation almost invented the word for *brutality* by the way it slaughtered its enemies and piled their skulls in the entrance of conquered cities. The Assyrian army combined efficiency with bloodthirsty methods to gain for itself the doubtful honor of being the best military machine the world had yet seen.[1]

It was for these individuals God called Jonah to go to and preach. For him there could have been no nation more revolting, which explains why he boarded a ship headed as far away as possible.[2] Finally after his underwater experience inside the belly of the great fish Jonah submits … goes to Nineveh to preach … and the entire city repents. Chapter 4 tells us Jonah's reaction. He gets mad and wants to die. There may be times we're more like Jonah than we care to admit.

Today, as we move *in* and *for* the culture, we will encounter those in need of rescue. We'll get to know unbelievers, people trapped in pornography, those struggling with same-sex attraction, women who have had multiple abortions, and people questioning their gender. How will we react? Will we keep the mission at the forefront of our mind? Preaching the ministry of reconciliation always involves making sure those in the world know we love them enough to show them there is a way out of their sin and that entry onto the road to forgiveness is always open. We must never come across in a way that communicates anger and hate. No one hated sin more than Jesus did, but He still wept over those who would be lost in Jerusalem … and so must we in the Jerusalem's of our day.

---

1 Grayson, A. K. "Assyria, Assyrians." Edited by Bill T. Arnold and H. G. M. Williamson. *Dictionary of the Old Testament: Historical Books.* Downers Grove, IL: InterVarsity Press, 2005, p. 100.

2 Jonah 1.2–3.

I remember the day in 1999 when the Columbine shooting happened outside Denver. I can tell you where I was as I listened to the news reports. My wife and I had taken some friends to Yellowstone National Park that day and were driving back across northern Wyoming to South Dakota as we listened to news reports on KOA out of Denver. We were all filled with stunned silence. We listened to every word of every report trying to comprehend the details. For days it seemed the entire country was in shock. Today, our nation has almost become numb to mass shootings. More communities than I can count are coping with the aftermath of these tragedies, including the one where I currently live in Dayton, OH. Once a shooting has happened, we all know the drill of how the media and culture responds. A vigil is held. A press frenzy ensues, detailing every detail about the shooter and his or her life leading up to what happened. Politicians and activists call for more laws. A week or two later, everything, for the community, returns to normal.

In all the mass shootings since Columbine until now, the reaction and aftermath of one should not go unnoticed. It happened in the Amish country of eastern Pennsylvania in the days and weeks after October 2, 2006. On that dreadful day, Charles Roberts walked into a one room Amish school and murdered 5 girls between the ages of 6–13. Then he killed himself. How the local Amish community went into action is incredible. Terri Roberts, mother of the shooter, described the grace with which the parents of the deceased reached out to her and prayed for her. On the day of the shooting one Amish man literally held the father of the shooter in his arms as he grieved. Thirty people from the community attended the funeral for Charles Roberts and soon afterward set up a charitable fund for the shooter's family since he left behind a wife and three children. One Amish woman told a reporter, "We can tell people about Christ and actually show you in our walk that we are forgiven, not just say it, but in our walk of life. You know you have to live it, you can't just say it."[3] The horror of this tragedy was just as real as all the others, but the loving, grace-filled response of the traumatized

3 Anne Curry. "Curry Commentary: Incredible Forgiveness." Retrieved 5/5/21 from http://www.nbcnews.com/id/wbna15134112.

Amish community stands out as a beacon of light. Christian principles were in action. *This is the way of Christ.* This is the ministry of reconciliation. We offer solutions. We don't build walls. We offer open arms—we don't make enemies. We live, in and for the culture.

MATTHEW ALLEN grew up in Malvern, Arkansas. He attended Malvern High School, graduating in 1992. He attended Ouachita Baptist University as an accounting major, before moving to Brownsburg, Indiana, in 1995 to begin training as an evangelist under Carl McMurray. Matthew received his BA in Religion Studies from Wright State University in 2017.

Matthew has previously worked with congregations in Tompkinsville, Kentucky, Brownsburg, Indiana, and Rapid City, South Dakota. He has worked with Cornerstone Church of Christ in Centerville, Ohio since 2010. Matthew has also preached extensively outside of the United States, by conducting evangelistic efforts in Belize (1998), Canada (2007, 09, 11), and Ukraine (2003, 04, 08). Since 2011, He has been making yearly trips to Colombia, working with churches across the country.

Matthew and his wife, Becky live in Waynesville, Ohio, and have two grown children, Emilea and Zackary. Matthew is the owner of Spiritbuilding Publishers.

Lecture 2

Raising a Christian Family in a Secular Culture

Mitch Stevens

Introduction

Before any kings reigned, God made a father.
Before any administration shaped policy, God appointed a wife.
Before any armies marched,
before any flag waved,
God made a family.
And it had enough trouble of its own for each day (Matthew 6:34b).

We live in strange times. Last year, when everything was shut down, and two weeks became month after month, it felt like we had the rug pulled out from under us. Everything ground to a halt. Whatever our families were doing, it all got canceled. For many years, modern families have been so scattered and divided from each other by busy schedules that most of their communications were through devices. And when they *did* talk, it was about figuring out the next item on the itinerary. Suddenly, with the lockdowns, the tables were turned. Those same families all found themselves close together under the same roof during daylight hours, and the virtual communication was with the divided and scattered outside world. I know some families, including my own, made some precious gains in those days. Our devotionals were longer and more regular. We ate together at home—we *had* to now! We took long walks. As we begin the long recovery, we want to hang on to those gains. Let's think about how to do that by looking at the word of God, applying some common sense, and using three images:

1. the **Garden** of God's intention,
2. the **Table** of family fellowship,
3. and the **Way** to daily go forward.

THE GARDEN:

Cultivating Loyalty to God (Deuteronomy 6:4–5)

The family is *the* fundamental human institution. A man's home is his castle. Marriage is his dominion. His family is his kingdom. The first family was planted in God's Garden, which tells us a lot about God's intentions for it. Our original commission was **growing and going**—be fruitful, multiply, and fill the earth.

> Therefore a man shall leave his father and his mother and hold fast to his wife, and they shall become one flesh (Genesis 2:24).

Leave, cleave, conceive, repeat. This is a naturally occurring process, but knowing we are images of God, we need to do it with spiritual intention. We must keep our home fires burning with the light of God in a dark world.

The Bible story traces the flickering torch of God's blessing for the family of man from the Garden of Eden: from family to family, to nation, and back down to a single baby born in Bethlehem, who left His Father's house seeking a Bride. At the start, Cain's family went astray. But then Seth bore a son. "At that time people began to call upon the name of the LORD," Genesis 4:26b. When the whole world became irredeemably corrupt,

> Then the Lord said to Noah, "Go into the ark, you and all your household, for I have seen that you are righteous before me in this generation" (Genesis 7:1).

When mankind again began to congeal into a rebellious mass, God scattered them across the earth and appointed the one family by which they would be blessed: Abraham's family.

> For I have chosen him, that he may command his children and his household after him to keep the way of the Lord by doing righteousness and justice, so that the Lord may bring to Abraham what he has promised him" (Genesis 18:19).

The story of Abraham follows a precipitous course as we trace God's promise in its infancy. Will it be corrupted by greedy alliances with the Canaanites? ("There goes Lot, off to Sodom!" "Will Sarah wind up with another man's child?" "Will this other woman's child fill in for the promise?" "Don't take that 'free offer' of land, Abraham!") The nation of Israel followed its own course of corruption, its own scattering, followed by God's reclamation with a re-emphasis on purified homes (Ezra 9–10). The Old Testament ends with families again in crisis (Malachi 2) and a promise left hanging of the Gospel Age, framed this way:

> Behold, I will send you Elijah the prophet before the great and awesome day of the Lord comes. And he will turn the hearts of fathers to their children and the hearts of children to their fathers, lest I come and strike the land with a decree of utter destruction (Malachi 4:5–6; cf. Isaiah 66:13; Zechariah 14:17).

The family, by God's design, is the institution by which all other institutions are made possible. In all times, it is our **Garden** to tend and keep. In evil times, it is the Ark by which righteousness is preserved. Growing and going

God knows how families work. There is no more powerful influence on the formation of a child's heart and mind than the household where he is raised. The flagship "raising a family" passage still must be Deuteronomy 6:4–9, Israel's #1 memory verse, the *Shema*.

> Hear, O Israel: The Lord our God, the Lord is one. You shall love the Lord your God with all your heart and with all your soul and with all your might (Deuteronomy 6:4–5).

There's the Garden—full immersion in loyalty to our God. The next verse concerns the transmission of that faith through the parents.

THE TABLE:

Time Spent Sharing the Faith (Deuteronomy 6:6)

> And these words that I command you today shall be on your heart (Deuteronomy 6:6).

When God built a covenant family, Israel, and Jesus took His Bride, the church, they both established these houses on grace and sacrifice. Then, they built an identity of remembrance and expectation around a supper time. The transmission of our faith happens around quality time spent together.

Why does Tiger Woods play golf? Why do Tommy Caldwell and Alex Honnold break records climbing up giant rock faces? ... Okay, that's all I've got for sports references. How about this? Why are my kids not that into sports except rock climbing? How are loyalties to sports teams formed? Through family loyalties—the influence of fathers and grandfathers. The late child and family psychiatrist Robert Shaw writes,

> If children's minds are like computer hardware, children's interactions with their parents (and indeed, with the world) are the software ... *Everything* we do teaches our kids something about the nature of life and how to be a human being.[1]

Research continues to confirm that "the most important social influence in shaping young people's lives is the religious life modeled and taught by their parents."[2] But this doesn't mean it's a shoo-in that your children are even going to maintain a brand-loyalty level of allegiance to the Lord's church if you put them in a pew three times a week. That will only have staying power if it builds off of the heart, with the very words of Christ baked into your family's daily habits. In the words of home and family lecturer Jim Burns, "Excitement for God and His Word is caught, not just taught."[3] That's where your true values come out, whether you intend them to or not.

> Keep your heart with all vigilance, for from it flow the springs of life (Proverbs 4:23).

---

1 Robert Shaw with Stephanie Wood, *The Epidemic: The Rot of American Culture, Absentee and Permissive Parenting, and the Resultant Plague of Joyless, Selfish Children* (New York: HarperCollins, 2003), 140.

2 Christian Smith & Melinda Lundquist Denton, *Soul Searching: The Religious and Spiritual Lives of American Teenagers* (New York: Oxford University Press, 2005), 56.

3 Jim Burns, *Teenology: The Art of Raising Great Teenagers* (Minneapolis, MN: Bethany House, 2010), 115.

What groundwater is feeding that spring? Parents, your faith is your children's hope. Your marriage is their sense of self-security. To prioritize these is to prioritize your kids' well-being.

Given the way it was designed, God warned us that "the iniquity of fathers" can stretch to the third and fourth generations (Exodus 34:6–7). We should have an equally long view while working righteousness in our families. We need to think generationally. "Where will this be in 100 years?" Bring up your children in such a way that they are thinking of their great-great-grandchildren.[4] While the world is only borrowing money from their great-great-grandchildren, we should be sending the word of Christ their way. When I say a family should be an Ark I don't mean we should be "bunker people." The whole biblical concept of heritage and inheritance is grounded in *optimistic thinking!*

Like the Garden of God, your home ought to be bursting with grace, love, and joy. Of course, every home will have off days and even down seasons. But a Christian home should be characterized as a place of refuge. There should be boundaries and structure—kids need those to thrive. The New Jerusalem has open gates, but it is a walled city. Boundaries set limits that allow free motion and safe exploration. Structure provides a means for safe experimentation. But if your house is all about nagging, threats, and ultimatums, the kids are not going to want to stick around. They will flee the Garden the first chance they get.

The transmission of our faith happens around quality time spent together. Much of that actually does happen around shared meals.

> Teenagers who dine regularly at home with their families are more satisfied with life. They are better students, are less likely to be sexually promiscuous, and tend to be much less involved with drug and alcohol abuse.[5]

---

4 Doug Wilson, "Postmil Parenting / Ask Doug," Canon Press, YouTube (Sept. 13, 2019).

5 Burns, 108.

Why is that? Here again from Dr. Burns: "Kids who have a strong sense of connection to their parents are less likely to indulge in at-risk behaviors."[1] So, if you don't already, work on building the habit of regularly coming to the table with your family to build positive experiences.

- *Let it be a time of debriefing.* Talk about your day. Listen to your kids. Be constructive but scan the conversation for key words. Affirm everything you can. This is not an interrogation, but an ongoing conversation in which discoveries can be made.
- *Let it be a time of storytelling.* Look for sermon points in daily events. Bring the words of Christ into play. Call to mind Bible characters and events. Speak plainly about the reality of evil and of Jesus' present kingship.

  O my people, listen to my instructions. Open your ears to what I am saying, for I will speak to you in a parable. I will teach you hidden lessons from our past—stories we have heard and known, stories our ancestors handed down to us. We will not hide these truths from our children; we will tell the next generation about the glorious deeds of the Lord, about his power and his mighty wonders (Psalm 78:1–4).[2]

- *Flow from meal to relaxed devotion.* After dinner, before dessert, read from a devotional book or straight from the Bible. This should be less formal than church-at-home worship. Everyone takes turns reading. Share observations. Ask questions of the text. Maybe chase a few cross-references briefly. As Tom Bunting put it years ago, make it "clear to every member of the family that in every activity there is recognition of God that affects our daily responses."[3]
- *Laugh and play together.* Make home a place where everyone can relax.

---

1 *Ibid.*, 110.

2 Tyndale House Publishers. *Holy Bible: New Living Translation.* Carol Stream, IL: Tyndale House Publishers, 2015.

3 Tom O. Bunting, "Worship in the Family," in *The Godly Family in a Sick Society,* Melvin D. Curry, ed., 1979 Florida College Annual Lectures (Temple Terrace, FL: Florida College Bookstore, 1983), 135.

> A cheerful heart is good medicine, but a broken spirit saps a person's strength (Proverbs 17:22 NLT).

If your table is not that kind of place already, make the effort. Think of it this way: If you started out as a bad cook, you didn't stop eating after one disastrous try. Grandma's biscuits didn't start as Grandma's biscuits. They started as hockey pucks just like everyone else's and then she kept doing it every day. You must take the lead with your attitude and keep plucking away. It's worth it. Unnecessary anxiety makes life difficult. The kids absorb it and send it back, and it spirals.[4] The cracks in the home where the world gets in often come from the stresses of overcommitment. "When a family is overcommitted, it quickly becomes under connected ... We have to learn not to prioritize our schedule but rather to schedule our priorities.[5]

"And these words that I command you today shall be on your heart," (Deuteronomy 6:6). Just remember—what is in your heart will be in your home. "The good person out of the good treasure of his heart produces good, and the evil person out of his evil treasure produces evil" (Luke 6:45). You're the chief programmer. You're the head chef. Bring them to the **Table** and share your heart. They're going to need strong grounding for where they're going.

THE WAY: Facing the World by Daily Sharing the Faith (Deuteronomy 6:7–9)

Everything is moving so fast it's hard to keep up. We can say the culture is worse than it's ever been in our memory. At this point, generations have been told by secular humanism, postmodernism, and recreational religion that they are nothing but particles in motion and that life has no overall meaning but that which is perceived by groups of people. Meaning is derived from groups of people whose only truth is what is true for them.

The systems and philosophies driving the culture today are fundamentally empty, and they are melting down before our very eyes. There's nothing

4 Burns, 104.

5 *Ibid.*, 97, 98.

like the pressure of an existential threat to bring out the true qualities of something. The souls inside these self-professed meaningless meat puppets are screaming out. The amoral culture is *exploding* in a temper tantrum of absolutist moral outrage. This actually gives us an advantage.

The first generations of Christians faced physical danger and official oppression. Historian Thomas Fleming scathingly observes,

> In our own age, the technique is vastly more subtle and more effective and more deadly to the soul. We are bribed with government grants and subsidies, teased by the pornography of mainstream television shows and the internet, numbed by prescription tranquilizers that our doctors are happy to give us, and dumbed by education and the media into believing in the myth of progress, that the world is always getting better in every way. [1]

I think he's right about the way it *has been.* But now, lines are being drawn. As the heathens rage, we seem to be crossing a threshold of persecution, from social ridicule towards official censure. I know with the rate things are going, we're still shell-shocked from having so completely lost the culture war, but we must resist the urge to "correct course" to get the gospel back into the mainstream before it can be seen as true and worthwhile. The upside of this cultural shift, I think, is that it will be harder to compromise and still call yourself a Christian. It will also make it easier for faithful Christians to draw back from secular culture.

This conflict is what Paul warned about at the beginning of his letter to the Galatians:

> Grace to you and peace from God our Father and the Lord Jesus Christ, who gave himself for our sins to deliver us from the present evil age, according to the will of our God and Father, to whom be the glory forever and ever. Amen (Galatians 1:3–5).

---

1 Thomas Fleming, "Winning the Marriage War," *The Rockford Institute Local Lecture Series,* June 13, 2013.

We must also reach far beyond the typical conservative impulse, which opines, "Oh, if everything could be the way it was ten years ago!" The erosion of the family structure in this country did not begin in the 1960s but was well underway in the 1860s.[2] We need to reach back farther to find our **Way**.

We must protect our little ones from exposure while we lay the foundation of a Christian worldview in their hearts and minds. One big way we can do this is to control their access to smartphones. Kids need smart parents and dumb phones. (I mean that only half-seriously. Well, maybe two-thirds.) Phones aren't the problem, peer pressure and cultural propaganda is, and that's what phones are loaded with. You wouldn't let a three-year-old play with a loaded gun. You might let them touch an unloaded one under sober supervision. The same care should go in dispensing technology in the home. Your child having access to technology is not a right, but an earned responsibility. Much is still unknown about the long-term effects, but this we know for sure: our ways of thinking and feeling and perceiving one another is affected by modern communication technology.[3] We are looking at each other through these filters and it changes the picture. It should be kept on a short leash.

First, exclude and criticize the secular culture.

> Since we have these promises, beloved, let us cleanse ourselves from every defilement of body and spirit, bringing holiness to completion in the fear of God (2 Corinthians 7:1).

We need to engage the culture's arguments. Their dumb idols will collapse if you just push them.

Second, fill your home with an awareness of the presence of God.

---

2 *Ibid.*

3 See Arichbald D. Hart & Sylvia Hart Frejd, *The Digital Invasion: How Technology Is Shaping You and Your Relationships* (Grand Rapids: Baker Books, 2013); Gregory L. Jantz, *#hooked: The Pitfalls of Media, Technology, and Social Networking* (Lake Mary, FL: Siloam, 2012); James P. Steyer, *Talking Back to Facebook: The Common Sense Guide to Raising Kids in the Digital Age* (New York: Scribner, 2012).

We must be constantly presenting ourselves and our children with counter-programming.

> You shall teach them diligently to your children, and shall talk of them when you sit in your house, and when you walk by the way, and when you lie down, and when you rise. You shall bind them as a sign on your hand, and they shall be as frontlets between your eyes. You shall write them on the doorposts of your house and on your gates (Deuteronomy 6:7–9).

Immerse every day in the presence of God. As Moses instructs, point Him out in the incidentals. Include Him in your daily habits. Adorn your words and actions with His. And build Him into the very framework of your home as you come and go.

> Through him then let us continually offer up a sacrifice of praise to God, that is, the fruit of lips that acknowledge his name. Do not neglect to do good and to share what you have *[our job is not just in teaching but doing],* for such sacrifices are pleasing to God (Hebrews 13:15–16).

To summarize, how you teach them about the world changes as they develop:

- from protection from the world to a controlled introduction and critique.
- from critique to preparation (they'll have to engage it at some point).
- from preparation to commission. The home, after all, is about **growing and going.**

It's time for your family to be the weird ones on the block. It's time for your voice to be seen as the stubborn, intractable one in the cultural dialogue. The world is rebuilding the Tower of Babel, and work has gotten far enough along that we can see it from our houses now. Perhaps it's time for our households to re-enter Ark mode. We must rally and tighten up our influence. Historian Thomas E. Woods has some good advice to this effect:

> Start with the people and places closest to you, where your actions can make a difference. This is the natural order of things. Cicero, like so many figures in our classical past, held that "the union and fellowship of men will be best preserved if each receives from us the more kindness in proportion as he is more closely connected with us." Paul says that "if any man have not care of his own, and especially of those of his house, he hath denied the faith, and is worse than an infidel" (1 Timothy 5:8). So begin there, with your own family, and proceed in concentric circles outward to close friends and local institutions that aren't destructive of every good and normal thing.[1]

> And whatever town or village you enter, find out who is worthy in it and stay there until you depart. As you enter the house, greet it. And if the house is worthy, let your peace come upon it, but if it is not worthy, let your peace return to you. And if anyone will not receive you or listen to your words, shake off the dust from your feet when you leave that house or town (Matthew 10:11–14).

Don't think of this as retreat or defeat, but rather as a reorientation. We can have a positive impact on the secular culture, but we must not fall into the grand delusion of top-down thinking. Woods continues:

> How do you hold on to what is good at a time when so many people around you, and every institution—including those you value, and wish you could still respect—have gone over to evil?
>
> It is up to us, in our homes and in our families, to teach and hand down those things that are beautiful and wise and good, to make contact with others who are doing the same, and to prepare the soil for better times to come.[2]

The **Way** we travel, after all, is a narrow path, not a superhighway. I have some experience with narrow paths. I like to hike. When I do, the occasional

---

1 Thomas E. Wood, "The only sensible next step for America," Subscriber newsletter, Jan. 7, 2021.

2 *Ibid.*

contact I have with other people on the trail is overwhelmingly positive. I definitely don't agree with everyone I pass on the trail. I know. I saw their bumper stickers back in the parking lot. I have radically oppositional worldviews from many of them! But just because we are interacting in a simpler place, over a common appreciation of its natural goodness, we have more pleasant interactions. In the same way, the workable way forward is to think closer and simpler. Your power to change the world is in your own home.

Conclusion

Raising a Christian family is about bringing your children to Jesus to receive a blessing.

> And they were bringing children to him that he might touch them, and the disciples rebuked them. But when Jesus saw it, he was indignant and said to them, "Let the children come to me; do not hinder them, for to such belongs the kingdom of God. Truly, I say to you, whoever does not receive the kingdom of God like a child shall not enter it." And he took them in his arms and blessed them, laying his hands on them (Mark 10:13–16).

This summarizes what we've covered:

1. God wants your family to dwell in a Garden of blessing: "Let the children come to me."
2. The time when your family is all at one Table should be spent facilitating that: "do not hinder them."
3. The Way you grow and go is as much a path of trial and sanctification for the parents as it is for the children: "for to such belongs the kingdom of God." And finally,
4. Anything that gets in the way of this makes Jesus angry.

So, come out from their midst and be separate, says the Lord (Isaiah 52:11).

MITCHELL STEVENS (you can call him Mitch) was born November 6, 1979 in Houston, TX. He was raised in a Christian family, spending most of his childhood living just north of Memphis, TN. He became a disciple of Christ at the age of 13. He graduated from Munford High School in 1997. Mitch began preaching full-time at the age of 21 for the Rocky Point Road Church of Christ in Cordova, TN. During his work there, Mitch received his formal education from the University of Memphis (B.A. in History, 2004) and Harding Graduate School of Religion (M.A.C.M., 2011). He currently lives with his wife, Kathryn, and four children in Dickson, TN, where he has preached for the Oak Avenue Church of Christ since 2012.

Lecture 3

Representing Jesus on Social Media

Keith Stonehart

Christian Introspection: The First Step in Reflecting Christ on Social Media

If glorifying God is our objective—then having pure motives is absolutely essential. We are all painfully aware of the many challenges, disappointments, and straight-up tragedies that have taken place with the onset of the COVID–19 pandemic and are still, in some regards, taking place. But when considering all that has made this challenging - have we considered how we as the kingdom might contribute in making the future better?

For example—how much of what we have endured was better or worse for us depending on how we handled the situation? And how did social media play into that? Could each of us do something different to better our situation or circumstance?

Let me say first that I think, considering all that we have endured, we have done remarkably well overall. Almost overnight, we had to learn and navigate through new technology to ensure that worship and study would still be possible, though somewhat augmented.

- We took time to hurt with one another and to celebrate where we could…
- We came together when it mattered most …
- We utilized social media and its varied platforms to teach, admonish, and encourage…
- We adapted and overcame…
- We found a way …

But now as we move forward, is there room for improvement? Or have we done everything right?

Certainly not.

The thoughts here are not so much geared to how we can use social media per se—as much as they are about how we may have been used by social media. For example, we must consider how it changed us... how we think... how we evangelize... and also, how we view ourselves. How has it illuminated the things deep in our heart that are necessary for us to change? Introspection and change are almost always necessary if we plan to continue to grow in faith. But sometimes, the ways we gauge that in introspection may fail us.

Take your nose for an example. Our noses fail us often, and we probably aren't even aware of it. Think about it—your mouth is right under it, but how often does it tell you that your breath is bad? Suppose you don't brush your teeth for three days—your nose won't tell you. Everyone else in the room will know you haven't brushed your teeth, but your nose will not remind you. Sometimes, social media is like this too.

It's easy to see what's wrong with every other person in the room—but it takes a great deal of observation to see what is sometimes wrong with us—even right under our nose. We must develop a keen sense of observation through introspection if we ever hope to improve and grow. The Bible both commands it and gives us plenty of examples of it.

So, let me ask you this: What is an inch? What is a pound? That's easy: An inch is a distance between two notches on a ruler, and a pound is a weight that makes the needlepoint to "1" on a kitchen scale. We take these weights and measures for granted, forgetting that they have no meaning and no definition in and of themselves. For an inch to be an inch, it must conform to an accepted measure. For a pound to be a pound, it must match an exacting standard. Governments have entire departments tasked with ensuring weights and measures are accurate, that they conform perfectly to accepted definitions.

Every human being lives according to a standard. There is an outside standard each of us uses to measure our morality, to weigh our ethics, to judge our successes or failures. We may compare ourselves to parents or peers or the great heroes of our childhoods. We may compare ourselves to the laws of the land or the laws of the universe. We may compare ourselves to religious leaders or sacred texts. But none of us lives entirely disconnected from outside standards, from some measure of comparison. We are no more independent than an inch or a pound.

As Christians, we are sure of our standard of comparison. We compare ourselves to Jesus Christ, for "whoever says he abides in him ought to walk in the same way in which he walked" (1 John 2:6). He is our standard. He is our measure. He is our criterion. If we wish to live moral lives, ethical lives, successful lives, significant lives, we must live as Jesus lived. He is our standard. But how can we know if and how we are "walking in the same way in which he walked"? How can I know if I am reflecting Christ on my social media? Through the Christian duty of introspection.

The Purpose of Introspection

The Bible mandates and models introspection. In Lamentations, we read: "Let us test and examine our ways, and return to the Lord" (Lamentations 3:40).

In 2 Corinthians 13:5 we encounter this command: "Examine yourselves, to see whether you are in the faith. Test yourselves. Or do you not realize this about yourselves, that Jesus Christ is in you?—unless indeed you fail to meet the test!"

The word examine is from a root word that has the thought of a "mine" or "mining" in it. To mine obviously involves digging deep below the surface in search of what lies beneath. It's hard work that is often very messy and dirty. There is little reason to wonder why then, in the Psalms, we often read of David looking inward and crying out to God for help in this task, Psalm 139:23. Asaph tells of the benefit that came when he diligently meditated in his heart and searched his Spirit, Psalm 77:6.

The Two Great Purposes in Introspection

The first purpose is to reveal sin. Self-examination is meant to uncover any areas in which we are failing to live in conformity to Jesus Christ. It reveals where we are withholding obedience and where we know the right thing to do yet are failing to do it. It also reveals areas in which we are relishing disobedience and where we are cherishing sinful deeds and ignoble desires. Finally, it reveals areas of complacency in which the Holy Spirit has revealed that an action or attitude is sinful, but we have not yet acted against it. It shows where we have not yet been conformed to the image of our Savior and leads us to respond in sorrow and repentance.

But introspection has a second purpose, which is to generate encouragement and delight. Even as we examine our lives for evidence of remaining sin, we are to examine our lives for evidence of God's grace. Christian introspection is not merely an opportunity to see sin and shortcomings, but also to see blessing. Self-examination is incomplete if it does not rejoice in commands that have been obeyed and sin that has been put to death. It is incomplete if it detects only failure and fails to see grace. For just as the evidence of our sin leads to sorrow and repentance, evidence of grace leads to joy and worship. Thus, there is both a negative and positive side to self-examination. Done properly, it balances sin and grace, and sorrow and joy, Psalm 51.

The Pattern of Introspection

Christian introspection is an important discipline for every Christian. Yet, for it to be effective, it must take a particular form. It originates and terminates at the gospel. It begins with the good news of Christ's completed work that has been applied to us. It is founded upon a firm knowledge that Christ has already borne God's wrath for our sin.

This means we are not searching ourselves to see if we have been good enough or become righteous enough to merit the favor of God, for, through Christ, we already have the favor of God! Rather, we are searching ourselves to see if we are honoring God and displaying evidence of his power and presence in our lives—whether we are *walking in a manner worthy of the calling to which we have been called,* Ephesians 4:1.

Having been founded on the gospel, Christian introspection employs the Word and Spirit of God. We acknowledge that in and of ourselves, we do not have what we need for accurate self-assessment, so we plead with God to aid us in this work. Our self-examination is truly an examination carried out by God. He is the one who shines the light of his Word into every corner of our hearts and lives.

Through Scripture, we search the inner and the outer man and cry with David:

> Search me, O God, and know my heart! Try me and know my thoughts! And see if there be any grievous way in me and lead me in the way everlasting! (Psalm 139:23–24).
>
> We plead, "Prove me, O LORD, and try me; test my heart and my mind" (Psalm 26:2).
>
> We join him in praying, "Let the words of my mouth and the meditation of my heart be acceptable in your sight, O Lord, my rock and my redeemer" (Psalm 19:14).

Just as introspection begins with the gospel, it finishes with the gospel. When we uncover failure, disobedience, and apathy, we plead on the basis of Christ's blood, asking, and receiving forgiveness through His finished work. Thomas Watson said this about our obedience falling short:

> Christ puts His merits into the scale, and then there is full weight.

When we uncover success, obedience, and zeal, we thank God for the gospel, which has renewed our will and given us a holy longing to be conformed to Jesus Christ. There is wisdom in setting aside times and seasons for diligent introspection.

We are wise to examine ourselves before we make major decisions and perhaps even at the beginning of a new year or a new season in life. We are commanded to examine ourselves before partaking in the Lord's Supper. But the bulk of our introspection comes during the normal routines of life. It comes as we read God's Word day by day. It comes especially through the preaching of the Word and is applied through meditation. Introspection is a daily duty.

The Fruit of Introspection

To layout only what the purpose and pattern of introspection should be, without describing what it looks like in real-time, would be nearsighted, as it would not describe either of these at all. While representing Christ in our Christian life is not a new concept, representing Christ via social media is. There are many trivial things that we may not have given much attention to before that now have become amplified and magnified in today's hypersensitive social media culture. For example:

- ***The Humble Brag***—"I am so very humbled to be voted best in my class this year."
- ***The Passive/Aggressive Response***—"You've done well for someone with your education."
- ***Gaslighting***—This is the ever-popular response to offense, for example: "Calm down; I was only joking ... Can't you take a joke?"

All three of these, by the way, came from one conversation with a relative of mine on a Facebook post.

If we are to represent Christ on social media, we must subscribe daily to the introspection we have described – but far more than that – it must bear fruit. Five questions we must answer:

As a result of introspection am I ...

1. Walking in the Spirit?
2. Bragging?
3. Envious or jealous?

4. Trying just to be right or win the argument? Or, am I seeking to save a soul?
5. Making the best use of my time?

Social media is robust with real-time engagement. Timelines are filled with reaction. Raw emotion and opinions are wielded like swords by political and popular figures alike. It's easy to step into this fast moving current and get carried by the flesh. Social media enlivens our carnality. We enjoy quick satisfaction. Emotion wants an outlet. Complaints must be heard. Anger needs to be expressed. And, contrary views must be vigorously opposed because that's what the flesh enjoys as well—superiority. This will mow down another's views—succinctly if on Twitter—while elevating its own, earning a satisfying flurry of shares and retweets. We all know how much the flesh loves validation. Walking by the flesh may be an accepted norm on social media, but it's not possible to please God in the flesh, Romans 8:8.

As believers, we're called to die to these carnal impulses and walk by the Spirit, especially on social media, given its reach and impact. We should ask ourselves if our posts are gracious and edifying.

- Am I slow to speak?
- Are love and kindness reflected?
- Am I blessing or cursing those I deem enemies?

Even when our posts are grounded in truth, our heart's attitude in sharing that truth is key. This is a daily battle; flesh against Spirit.

> For these are opposed to each other, to keep you from doing the things you want to do (Galatians 5:17).

This battle is amplified on social media, and yet, social media is where we can also shine brightly for Christ. We can point people to Jesus with the light of our lives, with eternal truth, and with grace-filled interactions. *People are watching.*

Conclusion

God both demands and describes diligent self-examination, and He does so for our good. It is through such introspection that we gain the true measure of our conformity to Jesus Christ. It is through such introspection that we can repent of our lack of conformity and rejoice in every evidence of God's good grace. It is the duty of every Christian.

So, as we look forward to whatever life brings after the pandemic, let's prepare ourselves with a little spiritual inventory. As you reflect over that time, ask yourself:

- Have I glorified God with my response to the pandemic, or have I just lifted my convictions above others in pride and faux superiority?
- Have I glorified God with my response to racial tensions, or have I dug my heels in the sand, refusing to be compassionate and rejecting the fruit of the Spirit?
- Have I glorified God in my response to the election and other political endeavors, or have I made idols of donkeys and elephants?
- Have I truly cared for others—or just myself?
- Have I truly made Christ the center of my life, or is that something I just say that I've done in name only?
- Do I accurately reflect Christ via my social media presence, or have I made myself my own God?

I don't know about you—but answering those questions might be much harder than it was to ask them. What will your answers be?

KEITH STONEHART began his walk with Christ late in his life at the age of 28. Having been the singer and guitarist for a touring rock band, the lifestyle associated with that profession soon took its toll on him, his marriage, and his outlook on life. Finding himself completely empty and at the bottom of a dark hole, in late 2001, he turned his view towards God and became a Christian after bible studies with his brother-in-law Mark Bowman who is an Elder at the Mountainview church of Christ in Cumming, Georgia, and Evangelist Brownlee Reaves. After years of intense and dedicated study, in 2009 he determined that he felt it necessary to get involved and give back by way of seeking the lost in the same way that he had been sought and began to work with addicts and married couples in crisis.

A year later he began to preach where he worshipped in Sugar Hill, Georgia, as well as a few other congregations that had no full-time evangelist. In 2010, he served his first weeks as a camp counselor at Florida College Alabama Camp where he met several members at the Fultondale church of Christ in Fultondale Alabama. A year later, after filling in for two weekends at Fultondale, he was invited to come and work full time with the congregation and has been there ever since. Keith now serves full-time in this capacity with his wife Kelly, his son Kole, his adopted son Carlos and daughter Kiah with her husband Ryan Graves.

Lecture 4

The Role of the Church in Society

Ken Weliever

Sir Christopher Wren was England's greatest architect of all time. There is a legend that when St. Paul's Cathedral was being built, a visitor walked on the site where three stone cutters were working. He asked the first one, "What are you doing?" He replied, "Cutting stone. I work four hours in the morning. Four hours in the afternoon." He asked the second man, "What are you doing?" The worker looked up, wiped his brow and said, "Just making a living. I earn six pence a day." When the third stone cutter was asked, "What are you doing?" He stopped. Looked up. Smiled. And with a wave of his hand exclaimed, "I'm building the world's greatest cathedral for Sir Christopher Wren!"

Many are like the first two stone cutters. Just working. Making a living. Doing their job. Then there are those like the third man. He was working for a reason. He had a goal. An aim. A noble purpose. Unfortunately, too many Christians and churches are like the first two men. They not only lack purpose, but in many cases, modern day churches have compromised their God-given role. Dr. David Jeremiah in a 2019 interview with Christian Post reporter Leah MarieAnn Klett, observed,

> Many U.S. churches today have "forgotten" their purpose, becoming entertainment-driven social organizations eager to blend in with secular culture instead of focusing on biblical discipleship.
>
> We're not an entertainment service; we're not here to see how close we can get to what the world does," said Jeremiah, the founder of Turning Point Radio and Television Ministries. "But there's so much of the world in the Church and vice versa that we can't tell a difference."[1]

---

1 "The Modern Church Has Lost Its Purpose", http://www.ThePreachersWord.com. July 23, 2019.

While I would have some theological differences with Dr. Jeremiah, I would have to agree with him that too many churches today have lost their way—their Divinely appointed place in the world. What is the church's responsibility and relationship in society? What is its function? Its purpose? Its mission?

Jesus died to establish the church. He purchased it with His blood. And He calls us together in it by the Gospel. Now what? What are we to be doing? How are we to be functioning in our current culture...or any culture?

This lesson seeks to answer those questions. Not in theory. But in practice. Not in generalities. But in specifics. And to provide direction for fulfilling God's desire and design for His people.

Fundamental Facts About the Church

People often speak of "my church," and usually we know they're referring to the congregation of which they're members. However, some folks act like it's their church. Like one fellow who wanted his way in a business meeting said, "I'm a charter member of this church." So, what? The church belongs to Christ. He promised to build it, Matthew 16:18, and purchased it with His blood, Acts 20:28. Furthermore, He's the head of the church, and the Savior of the Body, Ephesians 5. Thus, He has the right to define its purpose, authorize its mission, and specify its role in society.

Furthermore, we know that the church is a people, not a place. It's not a building, but a body of believers. Acts, the history book of the church, describes the church as a community of Christians, called out from the world and into a special relationship with the Lord. These verses speak of the church in human terms, referring to people:

- "the Lord added to the church" (Acts 2:47).
- "a great persecution arose against the church" (Acts 8:1).
- "Saul made havoc of the church" (Acts 8:3).
- "these things came to the ears of the church" (Acts 11:22).
- "Barnabas and Saul met with the church and taught great numbers of people" (Acts 11:26).

While some New Testament commands are collective in nature and others are individually addressed, all are about people identified as Christians and called into one Body, the church. We are the church whether we are assembled or unassembled. Saul persecuted and ravaged the church when he entered the homes of Christians and sought to harm them.

The various "one another" commands to Christians extend outside the four walls of the meeting house, and beyond our collective assemblies. While it is understood that there are specific commands unique to our local congregations, we need to realize our role in society doesn't stop when we leave the church parking lot. God's purpose for His people is revealed in His Word. It is illustrated in our fellowship with other Christians, in our family circle, and in our interactions with non-Christians in various social, vocational and community relationships.

And so, we come to the crux of the question of our study:

What is the Role of the Church in Society?

To simplify the myriad of exhortations, admonitions and commands issued relating to our responsibility in society, we've categorized them into three headings.

#1 To Follow the Example of Jesus

Christians are called to become like Christ. We follow His example, 1 Peter 2:21. We are created anew in the Divine image of righteousness, godliness and holiness, Ephesians 4:23. We must develop a spiritual attitude, Philippians 2:15. And we live, as He did, in the world without becoming worldly. It's a big challenge. But one, with the Lord's direction, we can accomplish. The basis of our role and relationship in society is encapsulated in the Second Great Commandment: "You shall love your neighbor as yourself" (Matthew 22:39).

Jesus lived in a corrupt culture, but He loved others, cared for them, and illuminated the Divine light of His Father in all His relationships, personal interactions, and social settings. He raised eyebrows, not only among the religious leaders, but at times among His own disciples:

- As He conversed with the immoral Samaritan woman at the well (John 4).
- When He accepted Zacchaeus' invitation to dine with Him (Luke 19).
- When He allowed the sinful woman in Simon's house to approach Him (Luke 7).
- And, when He ate and drank with publicans and sinners (Luke 15).

When He was challenged as to whether one should support the Roman government and its social programs with their tax dollars, Jesus commanded: "Render therefore to Caesar the things that are Caesar's, and to God the things that are God's" (Matthew 22:21). The church, both collectively and individually, is called upon to obey the laws of the governing authorities (Romans 13:1–2).

When we as a people become known as cantankerous, unreasonable, and contentious in our social interactions, we are failing to model the character of Christ. Have this attitude in yourselves which was also in Christ Jesus, Philippians 2:5, is an exhortation that ought to be demonstrated not only with each other, but in our societal relationships. The text tells us that Jesus possessed a submissive mind to the Father's will. It was also a selfless mind as He humbled Himself. He displayed a servile mind, that ministered to the needs of others. His was also a sacrificial mind that was willing to pay the price, regardless of the cost. And, in summary, a spiritual mind focused on the heavenly instead of the earthly.

The world needs to see Christ in us. In our communities. In our vocations. In our social clubs. In our schools. In social media posts. And in all our attitudes and actions. When we see our role in society as representative of Jesus Himself, we can then embody the essence of Albert W. T. Orsbom's beautiful, thought-provoking and life challenging hymn:

> Let the beauty of Jesus be seen in me,
> All His wonderful passion and purity.
> May His Spirit divine all my being refine
> Let the beauty of Jesus be seen in me.

When your burden is heavy and hard to bear
When your neighbors refuse all your load to share
When you're feeling so blue,
Don't know just what to do
Let the beauty of Jesus be seen in you.

When somebody has been so unkind to you,
Some word spoken that pierces you through and through.
Think how He was beguiled, spat upon, and reviled,
Let the beauty of Jesus be seen in you

From the dawn of the morning till close of day,
In example, in deeds and in all you say,
Lay your gifts at His feet, ever strive to keep sweet
Let the beauty of Jesus be seen in you.[1]

#2 To Model the Ministry of Jesus

When the disciples began arguing over who would be the greatest in the Kingdom, Jesus reprimanded them saying, "Whoever desires to become great among you, let him be your servant. And whoever desires to be first among you, let him be your slave." Then he reminded them that His ministry should serve as their model: "Just as the Son of Man did not come to be served, but to serve, and to give His life a ransom for many" (Matthew 20:27–28).

Jesus also provided a visual aid of what serving looked like when He washed the disciples' feet following the Passover meal (John 13:1–17). Although provisions were made for the meal, they had failed to either provide a slave to wash feet prior to the meal, as was customary, or do it themselves. Jesus, ever alert to opportunities to teach and serve, removed His outer garment, took a towel, and girded Himself, and washed their feet.

---

1 "Let the Beauty of Jesus," *Hymns for Worship,* R. J. Stevens.

Jesus' action taught the disciples a valuable lesson of humility. And that no one is ever too good, or too important to dirty their hands with the often messy and distasteful work of serving. Sometimes we must serve beyond duty. Go the second mile. And do more than may be required or expected.

Jesus also taught pastors and preachers an important leadership lesson. While we serve by leading, we must also lead by serving. Jesus' conclusion ought to hit home with all of us who wear His name.

> If I then, your Lord and Teacher, have washed your feet, you also ought to wash one another's feet. For I have given you an example, that you should do as I have done to you. Most assuredly, I say to you, a servant is not greater than his master; nor is he who is sent greater than he who sent him. If you know these things, blessed are you if you do them (John 13:13–17).

Often, we use the word "minister" as a noun. And more often, we refer to the preacher as "the minister." However, the word can be used as a verb. In fact, thirty-seven times the Bible uses "minister" as a verb that applies to all Christians.

The Bible exhorts: "As each one has received a gift, minister it to one another, as good stewards of the manifold grace of God" (1 Peter 4:11).

The passage teaches us three things about our ministry:

1. Our ministry is based on our gifts. We all have different "gifts." And they can be used to glorify God and serve others. The church family is a cooperative body where everyone has something to add. To share. To give.
2. Ministering is a measure of our stewardship. Stewardship is a Bible concept that says, "God is the owner. I am the manager." Biblical stewardship is a lifestyle. An attitude. A willingness to surrender to God. To give the best of everything. And the first of everything. This applies to my time, my talents, and my treasure. And it begins with an attitude of love. Love for God. And love for others. An understanding that we are

not just put here to consume resources. But to contribute. To give. To share.
3. We minister according to God's grace.

Paul put it this way:

> Having then gifts differing according to the grace that is given to us, let us use them: if prophecy, let us prophesy in proportion to our faith; or ministry, let us use it in our ministering; he who teaches, in teaching; he who exhorts, in exhortation; he who gives, with liberality; he who leads, with diligence; he who shows mercy, with cheerfulness (Romans 12:6–8).

We all have been blessed with different talents, gifts, and abilities. Our professions, personalities and personal pursuits lead us into to various opportunities to minister. By God's providential grace we've been provided a means to minister to others. Paul succinctly says, "Let us use it!" In the words of the 18th century Quaker missionary, Stephen Grellet, "I expect to pass through this world but once. Any good, therefore, that I can do, or any kindness I can show to any fellow-creature, let me do it now. Let me not defer or neglect it for I shall not pass this way again."[1]

#3 To Share the Message of Jesus

Jesus succinctly stated His mission when He said, "The son of man came to seek and save the lost, Luke 19:10. When His critics complained that He spent too much time with sinners and social outcasts, He related a trilogy of parables – the lost coin, the lost sheep, and the lost son—to drive home why He came to earth. That which is lost, needs to be found, restored and saved. And people are more important than either a coin or an animal.

Jesus' mission and message were people focused. He looked at those scattered and lost and felt compassion for them, Matthew 9:36. He saw in the rich young ruler human potential beyond the ability to amass wealth. Mark writes that Jesus saw him and "loved him." When He came to Jerusalem, His heart was broken because of their sins and wept over it. Not

---

1 Great Verses of the Bible: Galatians 6:10, http://www.ThePreachersWord.com. October 10, 2016.

the city. But the people in it. While healing people from physical infirmities, He often reached deeper in their spiritual lives and pronounced upon them forgiveness for their sins.

His message was the good news of God's love. It was the preaching of the Gospel and the power of faith. It included the requirement of repentance. And, of course, it involved baptism. In what we call "The Great Commission" given to the apostles, Jesus said: "Go into all the world and preach the gospel to every creature. He who believes and is baptized will be saved; but he who does not believe will be condemned" (Mark 16:15–16).

Jesus even used social occasions to build relationships where His influence could be seen and felt. We see examples with:

- Matthew's party (Luke 5:29-32).
- The Wedding feast (John 2:2).
- The Home of Mary and Martha (Luke 10:38–42).
- His acceptance of Zacchaeus' invitation to dine with Him (Luke 19:9).
- He ate in the house of Simon the Pharisee (Luke 7:36).

These and other occasions allowed Jesus to truly be "the light of the world" in a world darkened by sin. Today, we need to apply the methods of Christ when it comes to our mission, which is a continuation of His and the apostles' evangelistic ministry. The role of the church in society is not to be aloof. Or to be judgmental, condemning, condescending, or self-righteous. While there is certainly a time and place to refute religious error and condemn sin, we're sent to share His message of life and light to a lost world. We proclaim the Good News, offer hope, and to point people toward a right relationship with God.

Several years ago in an *Outreach Magazine* article, a non-Christian made this observation about those who tried to convert her. "I'd say 75% of these people don't really care who I am. They just want to build up their church or something. They don't even ask me what my name is."[1]

---

1 *Outreach Magazine,* "A Necessary Quality Overlooked in Evangelism," http://www.ThePreachersWord.com. March 1, 2019.

In the Barna survey,[2] 50 percent of non-Christians and unfaithful Christian respondents said they wanted to dialogue with someone who "does not force a conclusion." However, only 26 percent said that applied to practicing Christians they knew.

When you study the one-on-one methods of Jesus, He asked questions. He listened. He helped the prospect see where they were, and then gently led them to see where they needed to be. A wonderful example is found in Jesus' conversation with the Samaritan woman in John 4. While there are collective, organized programs, overseen by the Shepherds, through which we can participate, much of the work and fruit of evangelistic outreach is achieved individually. One person at a time. There can be no greater privilege, no more meaningful mission, no higher responsibility, and no purpose more eternally significant than the work of saving souls.

In an age when too many churches have abdicated their God-given responsibility in society by pursuing political agendas, questionable social justice issues, recreational activities, or even business enterprises, let's return the church to its eternal purpose. To the mission and message that God assigned it before time began.

Conclusion

The Greco-Roman culture of Christ's day was dominated religiously by many deities. When Paul went into Athens his spirit was stirred because of the abundance of idols he observed. Supposedly the ancient Roman writer, Petronius, once humorously quipped, "It was easier to find a god in Athens than a man."[3] Of course, as D. L. Moody observed, "You don't have to go to heathen lands today to find false gods. America is full of them."[4] Wealth. Pleasure. Power. Position. And prestige. These are all false gods in our culture

---

2 Barna survey, "A Necessary Quality Overlooked in Evangelism," http://www.ThePreachersWord.com. March 1, 2019.

3 Petronius. https://biblehub.com/commentaries/acts/17-16.htm.

4 D. L. Moody. http://christian-quotes.ochristian.com/christian-quotes_ochristian.cgi?find=Christian-quotes-by-D.L.+Moody-on-Idolatry.

that can lead us away from Jehovah God. But there is one more that Cal Thomas warned about in one of his columns. It's the false god of politics.

Apparently, some have forgotten in the heat of elections and partisan posturing that the answer to our country's problems and the ills of the world is not a particular political party. Or a specific candidate. Not long ago, I heard someone lead a public prayer asking God to touch the hearts of our national leaders to be guided by His Word. Then adding "so that we might be able to reach the lost." Really? I thought the power to reach the lost was through the gospel, Romans 1:16. I'm sure the brother leading the prayer meant well. And no doubt was concerned about the perilous direction of our country. Yet, the success of evangelistic outreach is not dependent upon which political party occupies the White House or is elected to Congress. The answer to what ails America will not be found in newly elected political leaders. Our real problems are spiritual. The root cause is sin. And the answer is Jesus Christ.

May the church of the 21st century see our message and mission as spiritual. And may our role in society reflect the purpose to which God has called us to hold forth the word of life, shining as lights in the midst of a wicked and crooked culture.

KEN WELIEVER has been preaching the gospel for over 50 years. He began as a High School student preaching on an appointment basis in Central Indiana and continued during his years at Florida College and the University of South Florida. Ken and his wife, Norma Jean, celebrated 50 years of marriage in August 2018, have lived in 7 different states and worked with 9 congregations including the Kettering Church in the 1970s. In June of 2018, Ken ended full time, local work to travel an engage in a national and international ministry.

Ken & Norma's travels and ministry have taken them to all 50 states, as well as Canada, Mexico, England, Sweden, Denmark, Kazakhstan, Greece, Italy, Israel, France, Spain, The Bahamas, Central America, and the U.S. and British Virgin Islands. Ken and Norma Jean are certified facilitators of Marriage Dynamic Institute based in Franklin, TN. Ken also has been active in Toastmasters and Rotary International through the years.

The Welievers' have two grown, married children—Kenny Jr. And Rachél Thompson. They are the proud grandparents of two grandsons, Roy and Miles and two granddaughters, Katherine and Fern. Ken has been publishing a daily devotional blog for the past nine years. You can read his posts at www.ThePreachersWord.com

Lecture 5

Love and Sex

Clay Gentry

We live in a sex saturated society. It's a major component to plot lines in TV shows, movies, and books. Sex is the topic of so many songs of every genre. Sexuality has become a political and social movement with gay rights and pride campaigns. Sex, through the medium of pornography, dominates the internet. Sports are being upended by transgender issues, specifically men competing as women. Storybook hour at libraries have been hijacked by drag queens. And let's not forget the ubiquitous ED commercials. I could go on and on but suffice it to say, sex is everywhere.

Yet, despite all the attention and even obsession devoted to sex, human sexuality sadly remains an uncomfortable topic of discussion among Christians. Consequently, and to our detriment, it is often ignored. This may be well and good for some, but how does this approach lead to a formation of a healthy understanding of God-created sexuality? I appreciate sensitivity surrounding the topic of sexuality especially in mixed company. These things are private and ought to cause us to blush when they are profaned and perverted, but not when discussed from a God-honoring perspective. We must talk about the issues surrounding sexuality. Why no sex before marriage? Why sex during marriage and how does sex solidify the marital bond? How does sexuality reflect the image of God? What about male and female genders? Why is homosexuality not God-honoring? If we remain silent on these issues, then Satan will speak. If we ignore these topics, then the world will fill the void. We can remain quiet no longer, we must break through any discomfort we might feel about honestly talking, teaching, and preaching about sexuality. Too much is at stake for us to remain silent.

Sexuality, From the Beginning

With that said, let's consider the question, what has God-given sexuality been from the beginning? Let's ground our response, and indeed our own sexuality, in what God has revealed to us through His word. For the answer, let's go back to the beginning, to the point in time when God created the first male and female.

> Then the LORD God said, "It is not good that the man should be alone; I will make him a helper fit for him." Now out of the ground the LORD God had formed every beast of the field and every bird of the heavens and brought them to the man to see what he would call them. And whatever the man called every living creature, that was its name. The man gave names to all livestock and to the birds of the heavens and to every beast of the field. But for Adam there was not found a helper fit for him. So the LORD God caused a deep sleep to fall upon the man, and while he slept took one of his ribs and closed up its place with flesh. And the rib that the LORD God had taken from the man he made into a woman and brought her to the man. Then the man said, "This at last is bone of my bones and flesh of my flesh; she shall be called Woman, because she was taken out of Man." Therefore a man shall leave his father and his mother and hold fast to his wife, and they shall become one flesh. And the man and his wife were both naked and were not ashamed (Genesis 2:18–25 ESV).

The "Helper" God Created for the Man

Alone, Adam was incomplete. Repeatedly throughout the creation narrative, God's work is described as "good" (Genesis 1:3, 10, 12, 18, 21, 25, 31). Yet, for Adam, his isolation and loneliness are heightened by the descriptor, "not good" (Genesis 2:18). So God paraded the animals before the needful Adam (Genesis 2:19–20). I have often wondered if this event was more than an exercise to look for a partner among the animals, but rather an exercise to demonstrate to the man that an animal, no matter how furry and cute, could not be a complementary partner. Nevertheless, the result was that after viewing all the animals, "there was not found a helper fit for him" (Genesis 2:20b).

To remedy the situation, God fashioned someone like Adam, but different from him (Genesis 2:21–23). Like Adam in that she was human but different in that she was a woman. Instead of going to the dust of the ground as He did with the formation of the man, God goes to the man himself and took a rib and fashioned and formed the woman. When God presented the woman to Adam (almost like presenting a gift) the man declared, "This is bone of my bones and flesh of my flesh; she shall be called Woman, because she was taken out of man" (Genesis 2:23). The mode by which woman was made informed Paul's call for the husband to love his wife as their own flesh (Ephesians 5:28–29, 33). What we have then, by the end of the creation account is that Eve (female) is the only sexually complement to Adam (male) in all of God's creation (vv. 23–24; also Genesis 1:27; Matthew 19:4). We can note here that God's creation and the natural order He put into place for human sexual expression, male with female, deems all other forms of sex as less than God honoring and therefore not good.

But more than just an account of the creation of the first humans (that was covered in Genesis 1:26–31), the extended record in Genesis 2 is the account of the creation of sexuality, marriage, and sex. This is about how we as humans came into existence as sexual beings. Moses interrupted the account that way, adding his comments at the end: "Therefore a man shall leave his father and his mother and hold fast to his wife, and they shall become one flesh. And the man and his wife were both naked and were not ashamed" (Genesis 2:24–25).

Coupled with the command God gave the first couple—"Be fruitful and multiply" (Genesis 1:28a)—it is abundantly clear that Adam and Eve are sexual complements and the sexual expression they enjoy together is good (cf. Genesis 1:31).

"Leave ... Hold Fast ... and Become One Flesh"

At the end of the account explaining in detail the creation of the Adam and Eve, Moses added a bit of commentary. "Therefore," he began. In other words, Moses is saying, because male and female are not the same making them sexual complements, then "a man shall leave his father and mother and hold fast to his wife, and they shall become one flesh" (Genesis 2:24). Based on the creation of Adam and Eve, Moses gave two imperatives:

First: A man shall leave his father and mother and hold fast to his wife. In Bible times, it was the norm for the bride to leave her father's house and come to her husband's family and home. Such as in the account of the marriage of Isaac and Rebekah in Genesis 24. What Moses is saying here is that a man should leave his parental relationship to form a new and primary relationship with his wife. Other translations say, "is united to his wife" (NIV), or "be joined to his wife" (NKJV, NASB), or "bonds with his wife" (CSB). (I'll admit that I like the KJV's "cleave" the best, mostly because it rhymes with leave.) Whichever phrase is used, the idea is the same, the husband creates with his wife a union that surpasses all others in its importance and permanence (cf. Matthew 19:1–9).

Second: They shall become one flesh. The idea of "one flesh" speaks of a complete unity of parts making a whole such as one God in three persons, or Trinity (as seen in such passages as: "let us" Genesis 1:26; "the Lord is one" Deuteronomy 6:4; "In the name of the Father and of the Son and of the Holy Spirit," Matthew 28:19). Thus, the marital union is complete and whole with two people who are similar "bone of my bone," but not alike, "man and a woman."

Furthermore, "one flesh" forms the foundation of a husband's love for his wife. First, speaking to husbands Paul said,

> Husbands, love your wives, as Christ loved the church and gave himself up for her, that he might sanctify her, having cleansed her by the washing of water with the word, so that he might present the church to himself in splendor, without spot or wrinkle or any such thing, that she might be holy and without blemish. In the same way husbands should love their wives as their own bodies. He who loves his wife loves himself. For no one ever hated his own flesh, but nourishes and cherishes it, just as Christ does the church, because we are members of his body. "Therefore a man shall leave his father and mother and hold fast to his wife, and the two shall become one flesh." This mystery is profound, and I am saying that it refers to Christ and the church. However, let each one of you love his wife as himself" (Ephesians 5:25-33a).

Here Paul presents one of the most meaningful and compelling descriptions of the oneness that should characterize Christian marriage. Following the example of Christ, a husband loves his wife with a sacrificial love of self-denial by placing the wife's needs before his own. Since in marriage two people become "one flesh," consequently the husband should love and treat her as he does his own body. Paul reasoned, a man does not think about loving himself because it is natural, so also, should the husband's love of his wife be something that is as natural as loving himself. Perhaps this love does not come as natural as we wish. Again, Paul offers the solution, "train ... to love," Titus 2:4. In context he instructs older women to train younger women to love their husbands, but we would all do well to learn from older wiser Christian couples how to unconditionally love our spouse with a "one flesh" kind of love.

Lastly, "one flesh" carries the idea of sexual unity. Together the man and woman complement each other sexually. It is in the marriage relationship the two are to find sexual fulfillment.

> The husband should fulfill his wife's sexual needs, and the wife should fulfill her husband's needs. The wife gives authority over her body to her husband, and the husband gives authority over his body to his wife. Do not deprive each other of sexual relations, unless you both agree to refrain from sexual intimacy for a limited time so you can give yourselves more completely to prayer. Afterward, you should come together again so that Satan won't be able to tempt you because of your lack of self-control (1 Corinthians 7:3–5 NLT).

It is the sexual union that places the couple's relationship in a category apart from any other human relationship. Moreover, sex functions to solidify the bonds of love in the marriage. A sexless marriage is a broken marriage. To deprive one's spouse of this fundamental marriage right is sinful and

dangerous. "Temptations to sin are sure to come, but woe to the one through whom they come!" (Luke 17:1).

"Naked and Not Ashamed"

The last piece of commentary Moses offered was a word about their nakedness, "And the man and his wife were both naked and were not ashamed" (Genesis 2:25). With no knowledge of sin and evil, the first couple's unabashed nakedness was shameless and innocent. It was not till sin entered the world that their nakedness was corrupted, and they desired clothing (cf. Genesis 3:1–7, 21). But there is also a sense in which their unabashed nakedness speaks to God's view of sex in marriage.

Unfortunately, most Christian teaching about sex generally focuses solely on the negative aspects of sex: avoiding premarital sex, adultery, and homosexuality. In these cases, sex is wrapped in shameful sin. This one-sided view of sex has, and can, affect many by saddling them with a negative view of God's great gift for married men and women. We should recognize that more space is devoted in the Bible to teaching on the delights of a wonderful love life than to any other area of marriage. In the marriage relationship, sex is normal, it is expected, it is something to be enjoyed, and it is something to be celebrated. For example, the Wise man counseled: "Let your fountain be blessed, and rejoice in the wife of your youth, a lovely deer, a graceful doe. Let her breast fill you at all times with delight; be intoxicated always with her love" (Proverbs 5:18–19).

This is no prudish view of sex. Later he expressed his wonder at the mysterious, intimate love between a man and woman: "Three things are too wonderful for me; four I do not understand: the way of an eagle in the sky, the way of a serpent on a rock, the way of a ship on the high seas, and the way of a man with a woman" (Proverbs 30:18–19).

But biblical sex is not only the purview of men. In the Song of Songs, we are presented with a collection of wedding songs capturing the erotic love between a man and woman. What is most amazing about the book is that the text is primarily female driven, not male. While both the man and woman passionately expressed their love for one another, it is the Shulammite woman who speaks more often about the delights of love and lovemaking. Through metaphor the woman expresses her erotic desires for her man:

"My beloved is mine, and I am his; he grazes among the lilies. Until the day breathes and the shadows flee, turn, my beloved, be like a gazelle or a young stag on cleft mountains" (Song of Solomon 2:16–17).

The promotion of female sexuality is also seen in Paul's instructions in 1 Corinthians 7:2–5 where he elevated the woman's desire for sexual pleasure to that of the man's: "The husband should fulfill his wife's sexual needs... the husband gives authority over his body to his wife" (vv. 3–4b).

The Hebrew writer stated, "Let not the marriage bed be defiled" (Hebrews 13:4). For the married couple, there is no place as sacred as their bed. The place where they can be naked and not ashamed. The place where they can enjoy the pleasures of marital intimacy. The place where they can escape the world with all its cares and concerns. The place where they can come together as perfect compatible partners in life. The place where they can be one. This is how God intended it to be from the beginning.

Conclusion

Few cultural shifts have proven so stark, and happened so quickly, as the attitudes surrounding sexuality in our country. Within a generation, ideas and behaviors, once generally condemned, are now not only tolerated but endorsed and celebrated by mainstream society. How did we get here? Not just as a nation, but as humans. How did God's "very good" creation of a man and a woman in a shameless sexual union go so wrong? It all goes back to the beginning when Adam and Eve first sinned. As a result of their sin, Adam and Eve were ashamed of their nakedness (Genesis 2:25; 3:7, 10–11). Eve's curse brought pain to childbirth and conflict into the marital union, Genesis 3:10. As a result, the course of human history has been one of sexual perversion, Romans 1:18-32. Nevertheless, as Christians, we do not have to follow the course of the world. We can choose a different course.

What is presented for us in Genesis 2:18–25 is the creation of the pure, uncomplicated human love and sexuality that God intended from the beginning. Sexuality is part of how God made us. When the Lord made humans, He made them male and female and He called it "very good,"

Genesis 1:31. As we've noted, sex was designed to cement the bond of a loving "oneness" in the marriage relationship. And it is in the intimacy of the sexual union that a man and his wife find unabashed pleasure in one another. This is God's beautiful design for human sexuality, let's not shy away from these Biblical truths but embrace them, share them, but most importantly live them out every day of our lives.

CLAY GENTRY works with the Jackson Heights congregation in Columbia, TN. He has been married to his wife Shelly for 21 years. Shelly is a reading specialist and interventionist at Columbia Academy. Together they have four very active children: Isaac (16), Lillie (12), Micah (8), and Anna (4). In addition to preaching, Clay is also a rural mail carrier with the Columbia Post Office. He enjoys seeing historical sights, raising chickens, a good story, and the occasional nap.

Lecture 6

A Christian and Transgenderism

Todd Chandler

2015 was a pivotal year in the cultural trajectory of the United States. Seven years earlier Chastity Bono, daughter of celebrities Sonny and Cher Bono, began transition treatments to identify as male with the new name Chaz Bono. Chaz produced a documentary of his experience, sold the rights to Oprah Winfrey and the film debuted in 2011. Over the next several years the media and politicians continued to promote transgenderism, so when Bruce Jenner publicly shared his decision to transition to a woman named Kaitlyn in 2015, the stage was set. In the months and years that followed Jenner received accolades from Teen Choice Awards, ESPN, *Glamour* magazine, Entertainment Weekly, *Time* magazine, and other high-profile sources and became the international face for the transgender movement. The same summer the United States Supreme Court redefined marriage to include same-sex couples. It was a watershed year for our culture, one that brought transgenderism into conventional conversation.

The transgender movement brings to the forefront practical and conceptual matters Christians must address: Where does a Christian learn about transgenderism? What is gender dysphoria and is it a choice? How do we respond to brethren struggling with gender dysphoria? What do all the terms mean in this discussion? At the time of this writing at least 20 states, the District of Columbia, and 85 municipalities in the US ban professional counselors from helping minors with gender dysphoria accept their biological sex[1]—how does a Christian a respond to those laws? Christians always are misfits in culture—hated, persecuted, wrongly judged (Mt. 10:22; 2 Tim. 3:12; 1 Pet. 4:4) and we must carefully consider our stand on the transgender debate.

---

1 Weir, Kristen. "A Growing Number of States Ban Sexual Orientation Change Efforts." *The American Psychological Association* website. March 10, 2020. Accessed 4/4/2021. https://www.apa.org/news/apa/2020/03/sexual-orientation-change

What you are about to read cannot address all the questions and I certainly do not know all of the answers. I am an expert in nothing and present this lesson only as my effort at an honest, accurate, and respectful study. I write, therefore, to people who accept the Bible as the word of God, believe Jesus is God's son, and recognize the depth of God's grace that sets us free.

Background

Gender dysphoria is real and is not a choice. For various reasons there are males who feel they should be a female, and females who have a sense they actually are male. It is a disservice to those dealing with gender dysphoria to dismiss or belittle their struggle as it can present arduous temptations, questions, and shame for which people need support. Like any other moral question, we successfully navigate it by the light of God's truth (Psalm 119:105), and the loving care of God's people (Galatians 6:1–2).

It will help to clarify some terms. I chose to present the terms as defined by the American Psychological Association (APA) and the American Psychiatric Association, two thoroughly secular organizations.

- **Sex:** Traditional designation of a person as "female," "male," or "intersex" based on anatomy (external genitalia and/or internal reproductive organs) and/or biology (sex chromosomes and/or hormones).[2] The website indicates an equivalent term is "gender assigned at birth." Note that sex is not real in itself, it is assigned. We should not gloss over this point, nor accept it.
- **Gender identity:** An internal sense of being male, female or something else, which may or may not correspond to an individual's sex assigned at birth or sex characteristics.[3] When someone uses the word "gender" in the transgender discussion this usually is the meaning.

---

2 "What is Gender Dysphoria?" *American Psychiatric Association.* Accessed 4/20/2021. https://www.psychiatry.org/patients-families/gender-dysphoria/what-is-gender-dysphoria.

3 "A Glossary: Defining Transgender Terms." *The American Psychological Association* website. September 2018, Vol. 49, No. 8. Accessed 4/4/2021. https://www.apa.org/monitor/2018/09/ce-corner-glossary. All definitions in the list except "sex" are from this site.

- **Gender expression:** Clothing, physical appearance and other external presentations and behaviors that express aspects of gender identity or role.
- **Cisgender:** Used to describe an individual whose gender identity and gender expression align with the sex assigned at birth.
- **Transgender:** An umbrella term encompassing those whose gender identities or gender roles differ from those typically associated with the sex they were assigned at birth.
- **Gender dysphoria:** Discomfort or distress related to an incongruence between an individual's gender identity and the gender assigned at birth.

Arguments to Support Transgenderism

We will consider three common arguments made by transgender supporters. The first is based in biology, the second in psychology, and the third rests in a philosophy. Biology and psychology carry a certain gravitas as "science", so I address each. However, our transgender moment[1] is the result of the more subtle but deeper revolution of an advancing worldview, and that is where lies the heart of the debate.

Biology

"I WAS BORN THIS WAY. I AM A MAN/WOMAN TRAPPED IN A WOMAN'S/MAN'S BODY."

What is sex? That question should not be difficult. Sex is central to the origin of humanity: "So God created man in His own image; in the image of God He created him; male and female He created them" (Genesis 1:27). This passage introduces the two natures of humanity, our spiritual nature "in His own image" and our physical nature "male and female." Maleness and femaleness make sense in our physical nature, our biology, only in view of sexual reproduction. The differences between male and female are far more than anatomical, but sex centers on the process of reproduction: "Then God blessed them, and God said to them, 'Be fruitful and multiply'" (1:28).

---

1 Anderson, Ryan. *When Harry Became Sally: Responding to the Transgender Moment.* New York, NY, Encounter Books, 2018:1.

The body clearly is organized sexually for reproduction. Male and female refer to this organization which allows an individual to engage in sex as an act. Dr. Paul McHugh and Dr. Lawrence Mayer speak to this point:

> The underlying basis of maleness and femaleness is the distinction between the reproductive roles of the sexes; in mammals such as humans, the female gestates offspring and the male impregnates the female ... This conceptual basis for sex roles is binary and stable, and allows us to distinguish males from females on the grounds of their reproductive systems, even when these individuals exhibit behaviors that are not typical of males or females.[2]

Reproductive organs have a distinct purpose and outside of that purpose the concept of sex simply does not make sense.

The distinctiveness of male and female extend well beyond sex organs, however. Space here limits this point but consider some basics. Humans have two copies each of 23 chromosomes; 46 chromosomes total, in nearly every cell. One pair of chromosomes determines sex. If a person has two copies of the X chromosome (XX) she is female, and if a person has one copy of an X and one copy of a Y (XY) he is male. Actually, the key to sex is a gene named SRY which is on the Y chromosome. If a person has the SRY gene, the sex will be male.

The impact of the presence or absence of the SRY gene is far more extensive than development of sex organs.

> Every cell has a sex—and what that means is that men and women are different down to the cellular and molecular level. It means that

---

2 Lawrence S. Mayer, M.B., M.S., Ph.D., and Paul R. McHugh, M.D., "Sexuality and Gender Findings from the Biological, Psychological, and Social Sciences," Special Report, *New Atlantis* 50 (Fall 2016): 89. Cited by Anderson, Ryan. *When Harry Became Sally: Responding to the Transgender Moment.* New York, NY, Encounter Books, 2018:80.

we're different across all of our organs, from our brains to our hearts, our lungs, and joints.[1]

We should not allow these differences to lead to harmful stereotyping, but reality cannot be ignored. In fact, when it gets down to medical matters doctors will take into account the biological sex of a transgender patient.[2] They do so because everyone knows that sex-based distinctions affect health care—because the differences are undeniable.

Notably, there are exceptions to the typical XX and XY chromosome arrangement. It is possible during the process of making gametes (sperm cells or egg cells) that the chromosomes organize improperly which can lead to an individual with abnormal chromosome arrangements. One may end up with two X chromosomes and one Y (XXY), or only one X chromosome. You will not see a person with only a Y chromosome since that genetic condition is fatal. It even is possible to be XX but have a copy of the SRY gene which moved onto another chromosome, in which case the person develops as male; or to be XY but have cells unable to react to testosterone and so develop female external genitalia but no internal female sex organs.

There are two key points to these aberrant chromosome arrangements. First, atypical sex chromosomes are a *disordered* arrangement which often negatively impacts the purpose of ordered sexual development. They are not variations of male and female or alternate genders; they are genetic errors. Second, abnormal chromosome numbers are essentially irrelevant to the transgender question.[3] The vast majority of transgender people have normal chromosome numbers; the movement is not about chromosome abnormalities.

---

1 Johnson, Paula, "His and Hers … Healthcare," TED talk, December 2013. Cited by Pearcey, Nancy P. *Love Thy Body: Answering Hard Questions About Life and Sexuality.* Grand Rapids, MI, Baker Books, 2018: 196.

2 Anderson, p. 85.

3 Anderson, p. 92.

So is it possible to be born in the wrong body? There is no conclusive evidence that there is such a phenomenon as having a male brain in a female body or vice versa. McHugh and Mayer studied this issue:

> Mayer and McHugh found that the gender identity studies focusing on the brain "have demonstrated weak correlations between brain structure and cross-gender identification." And the correlations that show up "do not provide any evidence for a neurobiological basis for cross-gender identification."[4]

We simply cannot find research data to confirm that this claim is viable.

The fact is that it is impossible to transition my biology, no matter what I think about my brain or body. An XX person is female no matter if she has a double mastectomy, adds prosthetic genitalia, and undergoes hormonal treatments. An XY is a male, and amputation of organs cannot change the DNA that affects every body system and cell in ways unique to males. Surgeries cannot transition a body to do what gives sex biological meaning—have the organization and function to perform sexual reproduction. No male can transition to be able to conceive and birth a baby—period. For Christians this should be clear: God made male and female and that only makes biological sense in an ordered design for reproduction.

Importantly, not only is the idea that a person can be born in the wrong body without scientific support, but it actually is disfavored by many transgender activists. This biological argument suggests that gender is determinative; that is, that biology determines gender. If a female can be trapped in a male body, then each of us is hardwired to one sex. If you pay attention to the current debate, however, you realize many transgender activists refute the notion that sex is biological at all. In fact, they remove the very term "biology" from the discussion so they can focus on their real belief – that sex is not determined by biology but by my mind.

---

4 Mayer & McHugh, p. 106.

Psychology

"I feel it in my mind, so it is real."

The American Psychiatric Association's *Diagnostic and Statistical Manual of Mental Disorders* published in 2000 (DSM-IV) termed gender identity issues "gender identity disorders"[1] but the next edition published in 2013 (DSM-V) changed the term to "gender dysphoria."[2] The change from "disorder" to "dysphoria" is enormous—mental disorders are something to correct in the mind while a dysphoria is something you can address by changing the body.

Recently, I searched the website of the American Psychological Association—apa.org—for "body dysmorphic disorder." The first result was an article addressing eating disorders including anorexia nervosa, bulimia, and binge eating. The other results included articles on anxiety, muscle dysphoria and cosmetic surgery. The first two paragraphs of the article "Beauty in the Eye of the Beholder" are telling (italicized words are my emphasis; not in the original):

> To the middle-aged woman seated in the office of psychologist David Sarwer, PhD, the scar on her face left from a childhood bicycling accident loomed large. She was often late for work because she spent so much time applying and re-applying makeup to hide it. And she didn't want to go out with her husband for fear that others would stare at *what she saw as a deformity.* But to Sarwer and the plastic surgeon the woman had consulted, the scar was nearly invisible.
>
> Sarwer *diagnosed the woman with body dysmorphic disorder,* a *mental illness* characterized by obsessive concern about a supposed bodily flaw that may not even be visible to others. The solution? *Not plastic surgery, but psychotherapy.*[3]

---

1 American Psychiatric Association: *Diagnostic and Statistical Manual of Mental Disorders, Fourth Edition.* Text Revision. Washington, DC, American Psychiatric Association, 2000: 535.

2 American Psychiatric Association: *Diagnostic and Statistical Manual of Mental Disorders, Fifth Edition.* Arlington, VA, American Psychiatric Association, 2013: 451.

3 Clay, Rebecca. "Beauty in the Eye of the Beholder." *The American Psychological*

In this case a psychologist recognized discordancy between a woman's mental view of herself and the reality of her body, and the ethical step to help her was not to change her body but her *mind*. You will find that is the treatment for all body dysmorphias.

Gender dysphoria, in contrast, is not treated as a psychological disorder. On what basis do professionals counsel patients, including minors without the need of parental approval, to undergo dramatically invasive therapies and surgeries instead of treating the psychological discordancy? There are differences between mental health disorders, but they are similar in the discord between physical reality and mental feelings, and it makes sense that the best interest of the patient is to help the mind fit physical reality. For gender dysphoria, however, psychologists changed definitions to force reality to yield to feelings. Addressing this point Ryan Anderson states, "Mental health professionals must not simply help people survive with whatever beliefs they happen to hold, but help people accept the truth, as they work through the deeper issues beneath the false beliefs."[4]

Unfortunately, that is not the tactic encouraged by psychology professionals. This is well illustrated by the "gender unicorn" designed by Trans Student Educational Resources (TSER)[5]; not a professional group but certainly in line with the APA. Notice that "biological sex" does not appear on the chart at all but is replaced with "sex assigned at birth" as though maleness or femaleness are things doctors simply construct on their own. The five categories illustrated can all contradict each other, but so long as people feel good, mental health professionals are supposed to support them.

Association website. June 2017, vol 48, No.6. Accessed 3/27/2021. https://www.apa.org/monitor/2017/06/beauty.

4 Anderson, p. 97.

5 Trans Student Educational Resources. "The Gender Unicorn." Accessed 3/27/2021. https://transstudent.org/gender/.

Christians know that the battlefield of spiritual matters is in the mind: "For the weapons of our warfare are not carnal but mighty in God for pulling down *strongholds* … *arguments* … every high thing that exalts itself against the *knowledge* of God, bringing every *thought* into captivity to the obedience of Christ" (2 Corinthians 10:4–5).

The truth makes us free (John 8:32), never feelings, and God's truth of binary genders (Genesis 1:27), is unmistakable in His word, *the* truth (John 17:17). Christians who stake confidence in His truth will see through the deception that says feelings are reality, and will help others see the truth.

Today, mental health professionals encourage school age children to cut off breasts and genitals, take puberty blockers to interrupt normal development, and undergo life-altering hormonal treatments from which they never can fully recover. No parent or health professional will encourage an 8-year-old to get a face tattoo of his favorite cartoon because he feels it is right, yet activists claim that same child knows enough about sex and development to submit to drastic treatments, and they make it look appealing with cartoon unicorns. For what demographic is that unicorn designed after all? It is absurd and an absolute failure to serve the best interest of people or lead children as God directs (Ephesians 6:4). Something foundational clearly changed to allow such a profound shift, and it is that foundation that we address next.

Philosophy

"I HAVE THE RIGHT TO CHOOSE MY GENDER."

As we saw in Genesis 1:28, the Bible teaches that we have a dual nature, a physical body and a spiritual soul. For Christians, the body is a "tent" that will be destroyed but our spirit will continue to live in a "house not made with hands, eternal in the heavens" (2 Corinthians 5:1). Though two distinct natures, the body and soul are unified. Neither the soul nor the body can be denigrated or made irrelevant to the other.

John wrote 1 John to Christians influenced by a worldview which taught a different version of dualism, known as Gnosticism. According to Gnostic philosophy, our physical and spiritual natures are divided rather than united. This means that physical choices have no bearing on our spiritual condition, and vice versa. One of the natural consequences of that philosophy is to conclude that the body (physical) has no relation to the true self (spiritual); what one does with the body is disconnected from who one is spiritually. 1 John addresses that error immediately:

> 1:6—"If we say we have fellowship with Him" (spiritual) "and walk in darkness" (physical) "we lie and do not practice the truth."

Discordancy between the spirit and body is evidence that I am deceived and living out a lie. Truth has been forsaken. Spiritual relationship with God cannot be divorced from my actions, my walk.

1:7—"If we walk in the light" (physical) "as He is in the light" (spiritual) "we have fellowship with one another, and the blood of Jesus Christ His son cleanses us from all sin."

Action that is concordant with spiritual reality brings those two natures into unity as God always intended. That is truth.

John further emphasizes this truth:

- If we say we have no sin, we deceive ourselves and the truth is not in us (1:8).
- My little children, I write these things so that you may not sin (2:1).
- Now by this we know that we know Him, if we keep His commandments"(2:3).
- But whoever keeps His word, truly the love of God is perfected in him. By this we know that we are in Him (2:5).
- If you know that He is righteous, you know that everyone who practices righteousness is born of Him (2:29).
- Little children, let no one deceive you. He who practices righteousness is righteous, just as He is righteous (3:7).

The Bible elevates and honors the body, going so far as to picture it as the most holy space known, the temple of God, 1 Corinthians 6:19. In contrast, Gnosticism was a deception that severed body and spirit: "These things I have written to you concerning those who try to deceive you" (1 John 2:26)—and degraded the body in the process. Gnosticism inevitably led to the erosion of morality. If actions do not matter to the spirit, how can anyone possibly think something like sin exists at all anymore?

The transgender movement rests on the same philosophical position, though the term "spiritual" is replaced by "mind" or "person". The current philosophy called postmodernism proposes a dualism which divides people into a body and a mind/person which are entirely separate.[1] We can think of it as a Neo-Gnosticism—I have a body but who I *really* am, my mind or person, is fully

---

1 Pearcey, Nancy P. *Love Thy Body: Answering Hard Questions About Life and Sexuality.* Grand Rapids, MI, Baker Books, 2018:14.

disjointed from it. You have heard that idea from all corners of American culture. Further, postmodernism states that each individual creates a distinct truth based on unique experiences, culture, and other influences. Because no two people have exactly the same experiences, no truth is more valid than another. To state it another way, each of us constructs our own reality from the pieces of our experiences. If we each construct our reality then it follows that I can deconstruct what others tell me is real and from the pieces build what I like. That philosophical idea is called, naturally enough, deconstructivism, and it is a potent part of postmodernism. You can see the appeal—I can make whatever reality I like and nobody can tell me "my truth" is less valid than any other. Nancy Pearcey discusses this dualism at length and explains postmodernism this way, "It treats the material world—including the body—largely as a construction of the human mind. There is no created order that we are morally obligated to honor or respect. Consciousness determines what is real for us."[2]

It is easy enough to see how this argument works with transgender activists. Anderson explains, "We live in a Postmodern age that promotes an alternative metaphysics. At the heart of the transgender moment are radical ideas about the human person—in particular, that people *are* what they claim to be, regardless of contrary evidence."[3] Transgender activists claim that biology is nothing more than a social construct which I am free to deconstruct and rebuild into what I prefer. The body is only what the mind/person says it is. Biology is irrelevant so if any discordancy exists between sexual traits and the mind, the body must give way to the mind. Anderson explains the significance of this sort of thinking, "This is a dramatic shift: from an emphasis on transgender identity being at odds with physical sex, to the idea of gender identity being essentially the *determinant* of sex; from acknowledging gender dysphoria as a mental disorder to regarding transgender identities as just a variety of normal human development."[4]

---

2 Pearcey, p. 165.

3 Anderson, p. 29.

4 Anderson, p. 28.

The body has a purpose from God, first introduced in Genesis 1:28 but further taught in the body of scripture. 1 Corinthians gives vital insight specifically related to sexuality:

> Do you not know that your bodies are members of Christ? ... Every sin that a man does is outside the body, but he who commits sexual immorality sins against his own body. Or do you not know that your body is the temple of the Holy Spirit who is in you, whom you have from God, and you are not your own? For you were bought at a price; therefore glorify God in your body and in your spirit, which are God's (1 Corinthians 6:15, 18–20).

This biblical truth of the body is where Christians stand. It clarifies the value of the body, holds it in esteem, and sets us on firm footing to deal with sometimes difficult questions about sexuality and identity.

Understanding the philosophy behind the transgender argument is critical. Nancy Pearcy rightly warns, "SOGI [sexual orientation and gender identity] laws are being used to impose a two-level worldview that disparages the physical body as inconsequential, insignificant, and irrelevant to who we are."[1] Such a denigration of the body has severe negative consequences because it is *unscriptural* and thus *untrue*. Pearcey continues, "This is a devastatingly reductive view of the body. Young people are absorbing the idea that the physical body is not part of the authentic self—that the authentic self is only the autonomous choosing self. This is ancient Gnosticism in a new garb."[2] Although this discussion is recent in our culture the philosophy behind it is neither progressive nor enlightened; it is ancient. Indeed, "there is nothing new under the sun" (Ecclesiastes 1:9).

Getting Practical

Human sexuality is complex, and our culture is in the middle of vast changes, charged discussions, and radical attempts to force transgenderism on us all, starting with the youngest school-age children. I do not have all the answers for Christians, but I offer some thoughts on how to move forward.

1 Pearcey, p. 195.

2 Pearcey, p. 196.

We must provide individuals suffering from gender dysphoria a place to find loving comfort and aid (1 John 3:10). It is a real illness and people need help from us, not judgment. John taught Christians to reject a disjointed dualism and to love. "In this the children of God and the children of the devil are manifest. Whoever does not practice righteousness is not of God, nor is he who does not love his brother" (1 John 3:10). Without accepting sin we must love those suffering with gender dysphoria as we would love and support any other.

Remember that human sexuality is more than biological (1 Corinthians 6:12f). Respect for the body allows us to accept the truth that sexuality has deep spiritual implications. We need to speak the truth in love on the theology of sexuality.

Christians should embrace biblical masculinity and femininity (Genesis 1:27). Sexual identity of male and female was part of what was "very good" in creation (Genesis 1:31). Pearcey explains, "There is a proper kind of self-love that comes from accepting God's love. A biblical worldview grants value and dignity to our identity as male or female. Gender theology is rooted in creation theology. What God has created has intrinsic value and dignity."[3] We should teach the differences between men and women clearly and without apology while avoiding inaccurate stereotypes which can trigger feelings of dysphoria. This is a whole set of studies all itself and we need them.

Respect 1 Corinthians 15:33—"Do not be deceived. 'Evil company corrupts good habits.'" Paul is not talking about friend groups, but wrong ideas. Postmodernism is a contemporary version of an ancient error and we had better respect its power to corrupt. In addition, Postmodernism is ubiquitous. Parents, guard against it and teach the truth of the unity of body and spirit. College students, be alert to its presence in every discipline you study.

---

3 Pearcey, p. 200.

Be ready for persecution and loss of freedom (2 Timothy 3:12). We in the United States have lived many generations without such a threat and though no one can predict the future, the verbiage in the U.S. is changing (Clay, *op. cit.*). Christians who hold firm to biblical truth eventually will be slandered, demeaned, and misrepresented and it is in those times we can shine as lights in the midst of a crooked and perverse generation (Philippians 2:15). We are, after all, "strangers and pilgrims" so let us exhort each other to have our "conduct honorable ... that when they speak against you as evildoers, they may, by your good works which they observe, glorify God in the day of visitation" (1 Peter 2:11–12).

Intentionally be "peaceable, gentle, showing all humility to all men" (Titus 3:2). Add to that, "gentle to all, able to teach, patient, in humility correcting those in opposition, if God perhaps will grant them repentance, so that they may know the truth" (2 Timothy 2:24b–25). This can be difficult on issues charged with emotion, but vital.

Pray (1 Thessalonians 5:17). It is the most powerful avenue we have.

TODD CHANDLER is the Associate Academic Dean for Student Affairs and Biology Professor at Florida College. He received a M.S. in Biology from Western Kentucky University; an M.Ed. in Science Education from the University of Florida, and a B.S. in Zoology from the University of Florida. He has previously preached at the West End congregation in Bowling Green, KY and the Livingston Ave. church in Lutz, FL. Todd and his wife Jeannie have four children.

Lecture 7

The Christian and Politics

Roger Shouse

The subject of the Christian and politics is one that generally comes around about every four years, at a presidential election, and a few comments from the pulpit are generically made about our responsibility and privilege to vote. But the past four years has changed all of that. Nearly every week, if not every day, the heated discussions of a divided country has been argued and debated on talk shows, newscasts and on social media. The rhetoric was often hostile and divisive. Riots in our major cities and the Capitol building illustrated how upset, and violent some have become regarding policies and politics. And this divide seems to have impacted the hearts of many brethren and even hurt the fellowship within some congregations. "I don't know how a Christian could be a Democrat," some have expressed out loud, while others have countered with how can you support such a vile man like "Trump." And this divisive spirit has spilled into the COVID–19 pandemic. Masks or no masks—some see this as exclusively health measures. Others have viewed this as a form of politics and yet another way to control people and even shut down churches. And this animosity has made some question the leadership of elders and has led some to even break fellowship and divide congregations.

Ten years ago, a study of "The Christian and Politics," would have focused upon the role of the government and the Christians responsibility to the government. Today, this topic takes on a whole new significance. Politics have affected our attitudes and impacted the faith of many.

Restoration preacher Benjamin Franklin wrote in 1856, "In every great political excitement, the cause of religion suffers in this country, more or less, in every church that has any spirituality in it."[1] Historically, brethren have been on all sides of this topic. Gospel Advocate editor, David Lipscomb, held the view that Christians should not participate in politics, including

1 *American Christian Review* (August 1856) 244.

voting, running for office, or being in the armed forces. Other brethren have held various political offices, including judges, mayors, governors, members of Congress and even the President of the United States, as was the case of James Garfield.

Our concern is not what brethren have done in the past but what doth the Lord require. What about "The Christian and Politics"? What are some things that we need to be reminded of? Throughout the Scriptures we find God's people in high governmental positions. Esther was a queen. Joseph was second in command in Egypt. Nehemiah was a cupbearer to the king. The Ethiopian was the treasurer to the queen. David and his descendants served as kings of Israel.

The topic of faith and politics is a relatively modern thought. For the first disciples, politics was something that they had no say in. Caesars, kings, and governors were appointed, not elected. Even throughout Europe, monarchs were chosen without the citizens having any voice or say. The establishment of this country was built upon the citizens having a say in who their leaders would be. This introduced a new concept, The Christian and politics.

The Lord was careful to keep His kingdom and His mission separate from the ruling government. *My kingdom,* Jesus told Pilate, *is not of this world* (John 18:36). Later, the Lord reminded Pilate that he would have no authority unless it had been given to him by God (John 19:11). God has been active in expressing His will through various governments. Joseph understood that it was the Lord who allowed him to rise to his position in Egypt (Genesis 50:20). Daniel tells us that the Lord "removes kings and establishes kings" (Daniel 2:21). Proverbs reminds us that the heart of the king is like channels of water in God's hand, and He can turn it wherever He pleases (Proverbs 21:1). The Roman church, sitting in the heart of the Roman empire, was told that the government is a minister or servant of God, Romans 13:1–4. God has used foreign powers to execute His will upon His people. The Philistines, during the period of the Judges, the Assyrians to Israel, and Babylon to Judah were all nations God used to fulfill His will. This remarkable history shows us that God is greater than any nation and His plans cannot be overturned by any power.

There are some principles that Christians must remember when it comes to politics:

God Is Our King, First and Always

Our allegiance belongs to the Lord before it does to our flag. That is true whether we live in a democracy like America, a dictatorship like communist China, or a regime such as North Korea. The wonderful hymn, "This World is not My Home," is a powerful reminder that we are strangers and pilgrims here. Our citizenship is in Heaven, Philippians 3:20. We do not fit in here and the world is hostile to the cause of Christ. God's people have suffered for generations through oppressive governments. This is true of Egypt. This is true of Babylon. This is true of Rome. The turning of this country will never come from the courthouse, state house or Whitehouse. You cannot force people to be moral, godly, or righteous. Change comes from within each individual as our hearts are taught the Gospel. We can be so concerned with right and left that we forget there is an up and a down. Our study of Scriptures has revealed two powerful thoughts for us:

1. **Kingdoms come and go.** Nebuchadnezzar's dreamy statue in Daniel 2 revealed a series of different kingdoms, one following the other. In the course of three verses, hundreds of years are covered. New kingdoms. New rulers. Yet, no kingdom is enduring except the kingdom of God. There may come a day when our country will no longer be a country as we know it. We may lose our independence. Like Judah in the days of Babylon, or the Jews in the days of Rome, we may belong to another nation. Our prayers are not for the endurance of this country, but for the kingdom of Christ.
2. **The people of God were expected to serve the Lord and honor Him no matter what country they were in.** This is true while they were oppressed in Egypt, captives in Babylon, or persecuted by Rome. When Jesus said to "render to Caesar the things that belong to Caesar," that included paying taxes that would pay the wages for the Roman soldiers

who crucified Him. When Paul and Peter told brethren to pray and be subject to the governing powers, that included those who were actively trying to suppress the cause of Christ.

Our hearts belong to the Lord. Lawlessness is never approved by God and it is one quick way to extinguish the light you are supposed to shine for Jesus. It seems that some get more excited about politics than they do faith. This ought to concern us more than who wins elections.

God Expects Us to Be Peaceable (Hebrews 12:14)

The suffering Christians were told to rejoice, not retaliate. Jesus told His disciples to turn their cheek, not to strike back. The Hebrews were reminded how they "endured a great conflict of suffering" including "being made a public spectacle," and "accepting joyfully the seizure of their property" (Hebrews 10:32, 34). They did this knowing that they had a better and abiding possession, v. 34. The great cloud of witnesses from Hebrews 11 each had to make difficult choices and endure various forms of suffering.

There are times when a line is crossed in our convictions and one must stand with the Lord and suffer what consequences may come. Moses' parents ignored the king's edict and kept baby Moses alive (Hebrews 11:23). Peter refused to abide by the order to not speak in the name of Jesus (Acts 4:18–20). These things are based upon faith and not what is convenient or what we like. We remember that the Revelation brethren who were facing death (Revelation 2:10) "did not love their lives even when faced with death" (12:11). The government may dictate that there will be no prayers, but the people of God will continue to pray. They could outlaw assembling for worship, but we will continue to worship. In Northern Nigeria, it is against the law to immerse someone. Brethren continue to baptize there. When at the crossroads of what God says and what the government says, we must side with God.

Consequences always follow. Shadrach, Meshach, Abed-nego and Daniel all show a stance against governmental rules that were contrary to faith. They also show that consequences followed.

As Disciples We Are to Walk By Faith (2 Corinthians 5:7)

Our politics do not shape our faith. It is our faith that determines our politics. Rather than standing with one political party year after year, the child of God must use his right to vote and consider which candidate will allow him to freely worship God and to "lead a tranquil and quiet life in all godliness and dignity" (1 Timothy 2:2). The difficulty for the child of God is that much too often, no one candidate stands out and shines forth what is right. It seems they all carry baggage that is troublesome to the child of God. Issues such as abortion, same-sex marriage, transgender rights, legalization of drugs are just a few of the moral touchpoints that today's Christian must think about. The issues of faith must rise above our thoughts about the economy, world affairs, the environment, and other social problems. First and foremost, we belong to God.

More Important Than What Politics We Hold,
Is Whether Politics Holds Us

The current nature of politics is mean and nasty. Wicked things are said. People are accused of all kinds of things. As disciples we must not get caught up in name calling, false accusations and manifesting an unkind spirit. The golden rule remains in place, even during election season. Kindness, gentleness, tender-hearted, doing good to all people are the core components of who we are. We must be more than careful what we share, like, and post on Facebook and Twitter. Some things are best left unsaid. One church leader said, "Wearing a mask will not get you to Heaven. Not wearing a mask will not get you to Heaven. But what you think about the one who differs from you may keep you out of Heaven."

The good Samaritan helped someone who was very different than he was. We must be sure that we are not walking on the other side of the road with the priest and the Levite. The color of one's skin, their politics, their education, where they are from should not factor at all into our compassion or our evangelism. Jesus went to Samaria. Jesus healed more than one Gentile. Among the chosen apostles were a tax collector and a zealot, opposites, but chosen and used by the Lord. Our fellowship is much more important than who is in office. Presidents come and go… good ones, bad ones, and indifferent ones. Yet, our heart always belongs to the Lord.

Conclusion

There is a thin line that separates church and state. Our government allows us to worship as we believe. State run religions is what fed the Roman persecutions and sparked the reformation movement. We appreciate not having to follow what outsiders tell us to do. But the other side of the coin is also a thin line. We must keep politics out of the pulpit. Politics in the pulpit ought to be like oil and water—they do not mix well together. There are principles that we live by and it is an honor and a privilege to be able to vote, but our major focus ought to be living holy and righteous lives and make it our ambition to please the Lord.

We are not physical beings who happen to have a soul. We are spiritual beings who happen to be wrapped in a physical body. While the environment, politics, and the world around us impacts us, they do not define us, contain us, nor control us. We belong to the Lord. Our ambition is always to please the Lord (2 Corinthians 5:9).

ROGER SHOUSE has been preaching the gospel for over four decades. Born a Hoosier, he has worked with congregations in southern Illinois, Indianapolis area, Kansas City, and for the past fourteen years in New Albany, Indiana. Roger is the author of Jump Starts Daily, a daily blog that is in its eleventh year. He and fellow preacher Jason Hardin host three weekly podcasts, *Heaven Bound.* Roger and his wife Debbie have four children and eleven grandchildren.

Lecture 8

Christians and Race

Max Dawson and **Reuben Prevost**

Is Racial Division a Problem?

The first thing we should ask ourselves is this: Is racial division a problem today? If not, we shouldn't waste our time discussing it, and we shouldn't waste our time trying to fix it. So, we need to ask the question. Indeed, racial division is a problem today. And we can see it in several areas.

We see it with respect to segregation.

While official segregation by race has been essentially eliminated from America, de facto segregation is yet seen in at least two areas in many communities. It is seen in housing in cities, both large and small. It can also be seen in our schools—many of which are underperforming—where kids seem to be trapped in a system that gives them few options or choices. While we do not turn a blind eye toward progress that has been made over the past several decades with respect to racial issues, neither do we turn a blind eye to problems and challenges that still exist.

We also see it with respect to the cycle of brokenness (also called systemic racism).

Ruby Bridges was the first black child who was allowed to attend a white school. She was five years old at the time and now she is 66 years old… Jim Crow and segregation wasn't that long ago. During that time, black men and women were sometimes thrown in jail simply because of the color of their skin, and their children grew up without parents.

Are we wondering why many in the minority communities are still broken today? Are we wondering why men of color are more likely to be deviant than white men? Are we wondering why men of color are more likely to end up in jail?

We've made great progress, but this is still a problem for us today.

Does This Have an Impact on the Church?

Our assignment is to talk about Christians and race.

Earlier, we talked about segregation in the world, but this is also an issue that we, as Christians, must address. It is still the case that Sunday morning at 11:00 AM is the most segregated moment in America. It is typically that way no matter what kind of church you are looking at. There are still some predominantly black churches that want to remain that way. And there are some predominantly white churches that want to remain that way.

We must ask:

1. Does that kind of racial divide please God?
2. Is it His will that races worship separately?

We already know the answers to those questions. Or at least we think we do. At this point, someone may say, "I don't see a problem." That's part of the problem. When people of a differing race are not welcome to attend and have membership in a church, that is a problem. We have heard people in black churches and in white churches say, "We like it fine just the way it is." You may like it, but is that kind of racial division in churches consistent with the will of God? We hope you know it is not.

And the issue is larger than segregation. There are times when men and women of color feel as if their concerns aren't taken seriously. There are times when they feel like white brethren are not sensitive

to their feelings and do not understand their culture. Here are some examples.

We remember when men and women of color voiced concerns after the George Floyd incident, but there were some brethren who brushed those concerns aside. They said things like "but wasn't he a criminal?" For men and women of color, it felt like some white brethren were trying to find ways to justify the death of George Floyd, or that he deserved the kind of treatment he got that day. While there may be very little overt racism in churches of Christ today, there are times when cultural and political differences can cause friction between the races.

Why Talk About Racial Issues?

The answer to that question is simple:

1. Because we want to solve problems in churches.
2. Because we want to do the will of God.

The problem that arose in Acts 6 about some widows in the church not being properly cared for was a problem. While it was not strictly a racial problem and was certainly not a black versus white issue, it was still a problem that had to be addressed. The situation would not get any better if nothing was done. The apostles were wise enough to look for, and find, a solution.

Problems need solutions. When we see a circumstance that is contrary to the will of God, we look for solutions. We can't solve all the ills of our society, but we can solve our own ills within local churches. We want God's will for our congregations. We want to operate by God's standards. When God's standards and our own standards are in conflict, who must change? Not God!

Racial issues existed in New Testament days. In John 4, the problem that existed between Jews and Samaritans was discussed by Jesus with the woman at the well. Jesus was as interested in the Samaritans as He was the Jews. Jesus presents a model that we should imitate. It began with a conversation—with talking to one another. How do you bring two people together if they never talk to one another? "The Jews have no dealings with the Samaritans," said the woman, John 4:9. She wanted to know why Jesus was talking to her! Why did He talk to her? Because she had the same need for salvation as the Jews. He talked to her because God loved the Samaritans just as much as He loved the people of Israel.

Talk is valuable. But we must do more than talk about problems. Like the disciples in Acts 6, we need solutions.

Can We Find Solutions to Racial Issues?

Of course, we can.

The place to begin is in the book of Genesis. There are two texts to which we might go for help. The first is Genesis 3:20, where Eve is spoken of as "the mother of all living." We have all descended from Adam and Eve. That means every man is my brother in Adam. To look down on another because he has a different racial heritage is to criticize God's handiwork. He is my brother from the same mother!

The second scripture is Genesis 1:27—"So God created man in His own image." Every human is made in God's image. Understanding this, believing this, and acting on this is the basic answer to all issues involving race. We sometimes wonder if we should even talk about "races" when it comes to the Bible. One mother, as she talked about how she was teaching her six children, said, "I teach my children that there is but one race—the human race, made in the image of God." Is that not consistent with what Paul said in Acts 17:26? "He has made from one blood every nation of men" (NKJV). The NASB words it as, "He made from one man every nation of mankind." Whether you say "one blood" or "one man," it still comes out the same. We all share a common heritage. We are derived from a common parent.

Understanding this truth is the most fundamental element in finding solutions to racial issues. God has the answer. And He is the only one with the answer. Politicians don't have the answer; through identity politics they often pit one group against another. Evolutionists don't have the answer; Darwin saw non-whites as inferior. Atheists don't have the answer; their beliefs would lead to the ultimate conclusion that none of this matters anyway—though they would likely deny that.

It is our contention that only those with a Biblical worldview know the answer to racial issues. Most people in our culture today say they believe racism is wrong. But if you ask them, *"Why is racism wrong?"* then how will they answer? They may have no answer. They may give you their opinion or maybe an emotional response, or they may even criticize you for asking such a "ridiculous" question. But only those who believe Genesis 1:27 know why it is wrong! If you do not have God in the picture, you have no unchanging basis for believing racism to be wrong. You may say you oppose racism, but you have no absolute truth on which to base your opposition.

The fix to racial issues is found by relying on God and seeing people the way that God sees people. It is evident from the beginning that God's vision is for all people to come to him. Isaiah said:

> This is what the LORD says: Preserve justice and do what is right, for my salvation is coming soon, and my righteousness will be revealed. Happy is the person who does this, the son of man who holds it fast, who keeps the Sabbath without desecrating it, and keeps his hand from doing any evil. No foreigner who has joined himself to the LORD should say, "The LORD will exclude me from his people," and the eunuch should not say, "Look, I am a dried-up tree." For the LORD says this: "For the eunuchs who keep my Sabbaths, and choose what pleases me, and hold firmly to my covenant, I will give them, in my house and within my walls, a memorial and a name better than sons and daughters. I will give each of them an everlasting name that will never be cut off. As for the foreigners who join themselves to the LORD to minister to him, to love the name of the LORD, and to become his servants— all who keep the Sabbath without desecrating it and who hold firmly to my covenant— I will bring them to my holy mountain and let them rejoice in my house of prayer. Their burnt offerings and sacrifices will be acceptable on my altar, for my house will be called a house of prayer for all nations." This is the declaration of the Lord GOD, who gathers the dispersed of Israel: "I will gather to them still others besides those already gathered" (Isaiah 56:1–8).

God wants the foreigner to know that there is a place in the temple for him. Even the foreigner is welcomed in God's house. We should never see ourselves as a white church or black church. "God's house is a house of prayer for all nations," Isaiah 56:7. Sadly, some churches are still thinking like the Jews during the times of Christ.

Lest we be too negative, we are happy to say that it is a new day among God's people. The old prejudices and biases are disappearing from so many local churches today. While we may still have a long way to go, more and more churches are welcoming to those of other races. Evangelism is thriving in many of those churches. The congregation of which we (Reuben and Max) are part is one of those churches.

How to Make It Work

See People the Way God Sees People. First, to be successful, we must see people the way that God sees people. Do we see others as created in God's image? When we do that, it changes the way we treat them.

When we see people the way that God sees people, we will listen to their concerns. We won't sweep them under the rug. When we see people the way God sees people, we will understand that other cultures are different from our own, and that's okay. When we see people the way that God sees people, we will work to address any problems between us. And when we see people the way God sees people, we will show mercy toward them.

There's much more to say about mercy, and we will come back to that idea shortly.

We Must Be Open to Racial Diversity. Second, to be successful, it is obvious that we must be open to racial diversity within the congregation. Teaching on the nature of the Great Commission and the value of every soul are critical toward achieving a congregation like God wants—a church that is welcoming to all people. That is the ideal, that no matter what one's heritage and ethnicity might be, such a person ought to be able to find a home in the local church. And it would be God's will that there be peace and tranquility as the congregation receives such a one who comes to Jesus in faith, repentance, and baptism.

Yet, experience shows that there can be misunderstandings and challenges in such an endeavor. We will make mistakes. We will sometimes say the wrong thing. We will hurt one another's feelings. Things like that will happen whenever we are out of our comfort zone. And, understand this, in a growing multiracial church a lot of us may initially be out of our comfort zone. Remember that the Apostle Peter made it clear he was out of his comfort zone when he first went to preach to the Gentiles, Acts 10:28-35. Out of his comfort zone, yes! But he had learned that "God shows no partiality." Understanding that truth will help make us more comfortable.

So how do we deal with hurts, slights, and disappointments with one another? And what if I have blind spots where I don't see how what I say or do might hurt another? Paul's counsel is the answer:

> Therefore if there is any consolation in Christ, if any comfort of love, if any fellowship of the Spirit, if any affection and mercy, fulfill my joy by being like-minded, having the same love, being of one accord, of one mind" (Philippians 2:1–2)

Things like mercy, love, and being of one mind are critical in overcoming misunderstandings and in dealing with challenges in our relationships with one another.

We will make mistakes. We need compassion, empathy, and patience.

> Therefore, as God's chosen ones, holy and dearly loved, put on compassion, kindness, humility, gentleness, and patience, bearing with one another and forgiving one another if anyone has a grievance against another. Just as the Lord has forgiven you, so you are also to forgive. Above all, put on love, which is the perfect bond of unity. And let the peace of Christ, to which you were also called in one body, rule your hearts. And be thankful. Let the word of Christ

> dwell richly among you, in all wisdom teaching and admonishing one another through psalms, hymns, and spiritual songs, singing to God with gratitude in your hearts. And whatever you do, in word or in deed, do everything in the name of the Lord Jesus, giving thanks to God the Father through him (Colossians 3:12–17).

This text is about mercy, forgiveness, and longsuffering. If my brother says something about which I might take offense, I need to be patient with him. He is learning and so am I. I cannot walk around with a chip on my shoulder trying to find fault with everything he says or does. Instead of being judgmental and harsh with him, I need to be compassionate and forbearing in my interaction with him.

The reason we do this is because we are all different people with different backgrounds, and we all carry our own personal baggage.

Because of this, problems and contentions may arise, but we need to show mercy. Like we said earlier, we are all learning.

Conclusion

So, how do we make a multiracial congregation work? We make it work simply by being Christians. By growing in those qualities that our Lord Jesus teaches us to have. We make it work by love. We make it work by being generous in our estimation of others and their words and deeds. We make it work by believing the best about others. We make it work by building enduring relationships with other Christians—no matter their background or heritage. We make it work by being what Jesus wants us to be. It is God's will that we be conformed to the image of His Son (Romans 8:29). To the degree that we do that, to that degree we will make it work.

From the beginning of the Great Commission, it was the will of Jesus that the gospel go to people of all nations, indeed, to every creature (Mark 16:15; Matthew 28:19). No one is excluded. It was God's vision that His kingdom be inclusive of people from every nation under heaven. That all peoples, nations, and languages should serve King Jesus (Daniel 7:13–14). We are subjects of that great king. We are here in our time and our place to make that happen. May our great God give us the vision, wisdom, courage, and strength to do that.

MAX DAWSON was converted to Christ by a co-worker at the General Motors plant in Indianapolis, Indiana where he worked in 1969. He was baptized by Mike Willis at the Mooresville church. He began preaching in the spring of 1970 and entered full-time work in the fall of 1970 at Noblesville, IN (1970–1973) and later moved to Kokomo, IN (1973–1978). Since 1978 Max has been with the Dowlen Road Church of Christ in Beaumont, Texas, where he has served as an elder since 1986. He has made eight extended preaching trips to South Africa, Zimbabwe, and Botswana to train preachers. Max is also the author of "Kingdom Leaders," a leadership training workbook. He has conducted more than 3,500 hour-long Bible talk broadcasts on radio from 1979–2014. He and his life Lee live in Beaumont, Texas.

REUBEN PREVOST was born in Southeast Texas in 1991. He grew up in Beaumont and attended the Dowlen Road Church of Christ during his childhood. Reuben was first introduced to preaching in 2007 when he worked with the Dowlen Road congregation as a summer trainee. He continued to preach on a fill-in basis throughout his high-school and college years. While in college, he met his wife, Ruth, and they were married in 2018. They had their first child in 2020.

After college, Reuben began preaching full-time with the Kleinwood Church of Christ in Spring, TX. He spent almost two years learning to preach and study in their preacher training program and is grateful for his time there. After training at the Kleinwood Church, Reuben returned to the Dowlen Road congregation as a full-time preacher. He's been there since 2019.

Lecture 9

Can Christianity and Science Coincide?

Dr. H. E. "Buddy" Payne, Jr.

The twenty first century has brought followers of Christ to a place where the question posed in the title of this treatise has greater significance than in previous generations, not only in western civilization, but in all parts of the world. Can Christianity and science coincide?

Christians in the twenty first century are living with a profound reliance upon the products of science in our daily lives—computers and other electronic devices, smart phones, robots, instant communication, instant access to information, convenient modes of travel, etc.—and with an omnipresent dominance of science in our daily discourse, as illustrated vividly in our dealings with the coronavirus pandemic.

The New Atheists have become more and more evangelistic in their attacks on belief in God and religion in general, claiming that science and scientific reasoning have brought on advances in our understanding of the natural world which have undermined the foundations of Christianity—belief in God as Creator, Jesus Christ as Savior, and the Bible as the revealed will of God.

Richard Dawkins has become one of the most successful and skillful popularizers of science in this century. As the professor of public understanding of science at Oxford University, he has often spoken and written to convince the public that the natural sciences, and particularly evolutionary biology, represent "an intellectual superhighway to atheism—as they did for him in his youth."[1] Quotes from him illustrate an extreme case of the passion with which atheists are attacking God and religion in our age.

---

1 McGrath, Alister & Joanna. *The Dawkins Delusion.* Downers Grove, IL: Intervarsity Press, 2007, p. 9.

> "If this book works as I intend, religious readers who open it will be atheists when they put it down. ... God is a delusion—a psychotic delinquent invented by mad, deluded people."[2]

> "Faith is blind trust, in the absence of evidence, even in the teeth of evidence ... a process of non-thinking."[3]

This combination of factors in our modern world can evoke a variety of responses in Christians, from respect and admiration for the amazing advances science has produced, to fear and distrust that science may overthrow the fundamentals of our faith.

Let's explore the question – Can Christianity and Science Coincide?

The Province of Science

Science (from the Latin word *scientia,* meaning "knowledge") deals with knowledge of the natural world that is based on careful observation. The scientific method is an empirical method of acquiring knowledge. Empirical evidence is the information received by means of the senses, particularly by observation and documentation of patterns and behavior through experimentation. Principles of the scientific method further involve:

1. Formulating hypotheses (reasonable explanations) by means of induction, based on such observations,
2. Experimental testing of deductions/predictions drawn from the hypotheses, and
3. Refinement (or elimination) of the hypotheses based on the experimental findings.

Clearly the methods and principles of scientific investigation are designed to increase man's understanding of the natural world. They have proved to be highly successful in discovering laws that govern the natural world and how to use them for man's benefit. A classic example of the use of the scientific

2 Dawkins, Richard. *The God Delusion.* New York: Bantam Books, 2006, p. 5, 38.

3 Dawkins, Richard. *The Selfish Gene.* Oxford, England: Oxford University Press, 1976, p. 198.

method is the discovery of the structure of DNA by James Watson and Francis Crick. (See the basic outline below, adapted from Wikipedia, The Free Encyclopedia, on the scientific method.)

Question: Previous investigation of DNA had determined its chemical composition (the four nucleotides), the structure of each individual nucleotide, and other properties. X-ray diffraction patterns of DNA had been made by 1939, but the technology was in its early stages and this research was interrupted by the events of World War II. DNA had been identified as the carrier of genetic information by the Avery–MacLeod–McCarty experiment in 1944, but the mechanism of how genetic information was stored in DNA was unclear.

Hypothesis: Linus Pauling, Francis Crick and James D. Watson hypothesized that DNA had a helical structure in 1951.

Prediction: Watson and Crick predicted if DNA had a helical structure, its X-ray diffraction pattern would be X-shaped. That prediction was determined using the mathematics of the helix transform which had been derived by others independent of the biological problem at hand.

Experiment: Rosalind Franklin in 1952 used pure DNA to perform X-ray diffraction to produce the now-famous photo 51. The results showed an X-shape.

Analysis: When Watson saw the detailed diffraction pattern, he immediately recognized it as a helix. He and Crick then produced their model, using this information along with other previously known information about DNA's composition.

This discovery became the starting point for many further studies involving the genetic material, and it was awarded the Nobel Prize in 1962.

Christians should rejoice in these kinds of scientific discoveries and should promote the study and use of science toward these ends. Scientists who were responsible for the development of the methods of science were, for the most part, strong believers in God who were convinced that a scientific investigation of the natural world was complementary to the study of Scripture because it was revealing the secrets of God's other book—the book of nature.

The following selected quotes from three of the great scientific luminaries from the days of the Renaissance show clearly how Christianity and science can coincide.

Johannes Kepler (1571–1630)—"I was merely thinking God's thoughts after him. Since we astronomers are the priests of the highest God in regard to the book of nature, it benefits us to be thoughtful, not of the glory of our minds, but rather above all else, of the glory of God."

> (Studies of the world using science are) acceptable to me and to Christians since our faith holds that the World ... was created by God in weight, measure and number, that is in accordance with ideas coeternal with Him.[1]

Robert Boyle (1627–1691)—"'tis like a rare Clock ... where all things are so skillfully contrived, that the Engine being once set a Moving, all things proceed according to the Artificers ... design."[2]

> The Wise Author of Nature has so excellently Contriv'd the Universe, that the more Clearly and Particularly we Discern, how Congruous the Means are to the Ends to be obtain'd by them, the more Plainly we Discern the Admirable Wisdom of the Omniscient

1 Kepler, Johannes with E. J. Aiton, A. M. Duncan, and J. V. Field, trans., *The Harmony of the World.* Philadelphia: American Philosophical Society, 1997.

2 Russell, Colin A. "The Conflict of Science and Religion." *Science and Religion: A Historical Introduction.* Edited by Gary B. Ferguson, pp. 3–12. Baltimore: Johns Hopkins Univ. Press, 2002. p. 4.

Author of Things; of whom it is Truly said by a Prophet (Isaiah), *that He is Wonderful in Counsel, and Excellent in Working.*[1]

Isaac Newton (1642–1727)—"Though these bodies may indeed continue in their orbits by the mere laws of gravity, yet they could by no means have at first derived the regular position of the orbits themselves from these laws. Thus, this most beautiful system of the sun, planets, and comets, could only proceed from the council and dominion of an intelligent and powerful Being" *(General Scholium to the* Principia, appendix to the second edition of 1713).[2]

While the methods of science *cannot* be used to directly investigate the areas of knowledge involving the immaterial, the spiritual, or the supernatural because these cannot be observed by the senses, reasonable inferences can sometimes be drawn about these areas of knowledge based on empirical evidence obtained from the observations of science. However, there is a limit to what science can tell us in these realms.

A classic example of using the scientific method in this way is the famous Argument from Design, an argument which Richard Dawkins described as "always the most influential of the arguments for the existence of a God"[3]—an argument which is supported by Scripture as well.

The Argument from Design

God Himself appeals to this kind of reasoning in Scripture (see the two key Scriptures below). He declares in these and other Scriptures that He has given a testimony to Himself in the features of the natural world. Man can

---

1 Boyle, Robert. "A Disquisition about the Final Causes of Natural Things." *The Works of Robert Boyle,* edited by Edward B. Davis and Michael Hunter. 14 volumes, 11:79–152. London: Pickering and Chatto, 1999–2000. pp. 150–51.

2 Newton, Isaac. *The Principia, Mathematical principles of natural philosophy,* a new translation by I. Bernard Cohen and Anne Whitman, preceded by "A Guide to Newton's Principia" by I. Bernard Cohen. Oakland, California: University of California Press, 1999.

3 Dawkins, Richard. *The Blind Watchmaker.* New York: W.W. Norton & Company, 1987, p. 4.

observe design in nature and can reasonably conclude that there must have been a Grand Designer.

> The heavens declare the glory of God; and the firmament shows His handiwork. Day unto day utters speech, and night unto night reveals knowledge. There is no speech nor language where their voice is not heard. Their line has gone out through all the earth, and their words to the end of the world (Psalm 19:1–4a).

> For since the creation of the world His invisible attributes are clearly seen, being understood by the things that are made, even His eternal power and Godhead, so that they are without excuse (Romans 1:20).

Prior to the late nineteenth century, the dominant worldview, even among intellectuals as illustrated in the quotes above from Kepler, Boyle, and Newton, was that the testimony of nature supported Scripture in declaring that the world was created by God. William Paley's (1743–1805) book, *Natural Theology; or Evidences of the Existence and Attributes of the Deity* published in 1802 and republished many times since, became a standard work read by university students around the western world, including Charles Darwin who claimed he found Paley's arguments conclusive in his earlier life. He begins that famous treatise with the following, which represents well the argument from design:

> In crossing a heath, suppose I pitched my foot against a stone, and were asked how the stone came to be there; I might possibly answer, that, for anything I knew to the contrary, it had lain there forever: nor would it perhaps be very easy to show the absurdity of this answer. But suppose I had found a watch upon the ground, and it should be inquired how the watch happened to be in that place; I should hardly think of the answer which I had before given, that for anything I knew, the watch might have always been there ... the watch must have had a maker: ... who comprehended its construction, and designed its use ... every manifestation of design,

> which existed in the watch, exists in the works of nature, with the difference, on the side of nature, of being greater or more, and that in a degree which exceeds all computation.[1]

Over the course of the nineteenth and twentieth centuries, the dominant worldview changed dramatically. By the end of the twentieth century the widely accepted worldview, especially among the leaders of the scientific community, was that of scientific materialism—a view expressed succinctly by Carl Sagan in his popular Cosmos series—"The Cosmos is all that is or was or ever will be." The argument from design fell into disfavor because, in the view of the materialists, nature itself can produce the appearance of design, and thus there is no need for a Designer.

The history of this dramatic shift demands much more explanation than the present treatise allows, but the work of several key scientists certainly played major roles.

1. **Pierre-Simon de La Place (1749–1827)**—argued in his five-volume Celestial Mechanics (published between 1799 and 1825)[2] that nature with its matter, energy and forces could produce and maintain our solar system—*there was no need for a God hypothesis as Newton had so eloquently argued.* Or as Richard Dawkins would later say: "The universe we observe has precisely the properties we should expect if there is at bottom, no design, no purpose, no evil, no good, nothing but blind, pitiless indifference."[3]
2. **Charles Lyell (1797–1875)**—proposed in his *Principles of Geology* (published between 1830 and 1833) that Earth and all its geologic features were shaped by the same natural processes still in operation

1 Paley, William. *Natural Theology; or Evidences for the Existence and Attributes of the Deity.* London: R. Faulder, 1802.

2 Laplace, Pierre-Simon with Mary Somerville, trans., *Mechanism of the Heavens.* London: John Murray, 1831.

3 Dawkins, Richard. *River Out of Eden: A Darwinian View of Life.* New York: Basic Books, 1995, p. 133.

today over long periods of time[4]—*there was no need for intervention by God.*

3. **Charles Darwin (1809–1882)**—argued in his world-changing volume *On the Origin of Species* (published in 1859)[5] that populations evolve over the course of generations through a process of natural selection acting on natural variation; that the diversity of life arose by common descent through a branching pattern of evolution—*there was no need for a Designer to account for the origin of the species of life.* Or as Douglas Futuyma would later say: "By coupling the undirected, purposeless variations to the blind, uncaring process of natural selection, Darwin made the theological or spiritual explanations of the life processes superfluous."[6]
4. **A.I. Oparin (1894–1980)** and **J.B.S. Haldane (1892–1964)** independently proposed (in the 1920s) the hypothesis that the early earth had a reducing atmosphere which could have allowed the production of the primary building blocks of life leading to a "primordial soup" and ultimately the origin of first life on earth by natural causes. **Stanley Miller (1930–2007)** and **Harold Urey (1893–1981)** devised an experiment to test this hypothesis (published in *Science* in 1953), and thereby produced a few the basic building blocks for life by natural causes—*there was no need for God to produce life.*

The evolutionary worldview had won the day. The solar system had evolved by natural causes from eternally existent matter and energy; the geologic features of earth had come about by natural causes; living species had originated by natural selection acting on natural variation; and life itself could have originated by natural causes. While there was an appearance of design in some instances, these could be explained by natural causes. The materialist worldview became the new paradigm.

---

4 Lyell, Charles. *Principles of Geology.* (Cambridge Library Collection—Earth Science), Cambridge: Cambridge University Press, 2009.

5 Darwin, Charles. *On the Origin of Species by Means of Natural Selection.* New York: Penguin Books, 1968.

6 Futuyma, Douglas J. *Evolutionary Biology* (3rd Ed.). Sunderland, MA: Sinauer Associates, 1998. p. 3.

Every discipline of the standard college curriculum was profoundly affected by this worldview. My experience as a Christian and a college student at Florida State University and Harvard University in the 1960s was not uncommon. Professors would affirm that the sciences had demonstrated the evolutionary worldview beyond question. They would challenge believers in God to stop believing in myths. I was not prepared to answer these challenges and the scientific materials I found supporting the view that God created the universe, the Earth and life were weak at best.

My experience was and is representative of many other college students, many of whom have come to question whether Christianity and science can coincide. It was that very experience that led me to spend the last fifty years of my life with the avowed purpose of studying scientific evidences deeply to answer the question, "Is it reasonable to believe in God in this scientific age?" With the explosion of scientific discovery in the twentieth and twenty first centuries, can an honest-minded seeker still declare with the Psalmist, "The heavens declare the glory of God?" My message to Christians, young and old, is that you need have no fear of the sciences. In every generation God has provided sufficient evidence in the things that are made to lead you to faith in Him. It need not and should not be "blind faith"!

While there will always remain unanswered questions sufficient to require any position on origins to be a position of faith (we will always have to *believe* that God is—Hebrew 11:6), I will close out this treatise by sharing with the readers a glimpse into some amazing scientific discoveries over the last 100 years that have led a good number of unbelievers to become believers in a Grand Designer, despite the dominant materialist worldview. It is truly the argument from design revisited.

The Argument from Design Revisited

First, it has become convincingly evident that the universe had a beginning. For the sake of space, I am purposely providing only the briefest of explanations for this first point.

If the Cosmos is all there is or ever has been, as Carl Sagan famously proclaimed, then clearly it must have always been in existence. Its matter and energy produced all we observe today by natural causes, but the matter and energy themselves are eternal. However, several discoveries in the last 100 years led physicists to believe that the preponderance of the evidence points to a universe that had a beginning.

1. The following discoveries by astronomer Edwin Hubble (1889–1953) at the Mt. Wilson Observatory in the 1920s led to the theory that the universe is expanding.
   a. Many objects previously thought to be clouds of dust and gas and classified as "nebulae" were actually galaxies beyond the Milky Way.
   b. Those galaxies were traveling away from Earth, as indicated by the red shift of light coming from those galaxies, and the recessional velocity of a galaxy increases with its distance from the Earth.
2. Albert Einstein's theory of relativity led him to the conclusion that the universe must be either expanding or contracting. Unable to believe his own equations, he introduced what he called a cosmological constant to offset the necessary conclusion that the universe is not eternal. Upon finding out about Hubble's red shift evidence of expansion, Einstein (and many others) clearly saw that an expanding universe declares the need for a *beginning* and called his introduction of a cosmological constant the "greatest blunder of his life."
3. Allan Sandage (1926–2010), a graduate assistant to Edwin Hubble in the early 1950s, continued Hubble's research program as an astronomer with the Carnegie Institute Observatories for over 50 years. In 1985, at the age of 59, during a conference in Dallas on the origin of the universe, life, and consciousness, he sat on a panel with the theists rather than the non-theists and declared:
   a. That science had taken us to the "first event", but it could not take us further to the "first cause"—the most reasonable explanation of which is God.
   b. The sudden emergence of matter, space, time, and energy pointed the need for some kind of transcendence—something beyond nature.

c. "Here is evidence for what can only be described as a supernatural event. There is no way that this could have been predicted within the realm of physics as we know it."[1]
d. Sandage saw that the scientific materialist's worldview cannot explain this scientific evidence.

Second, the evidence has become overwhelming that the universe, our solar system, and this Earth are remarkably fine-tuned to support life on Earth and have been since the beginning.

Paul Davies in his book *The Goldilocks Enigma: Why is the Universe Just Right for Life?* makes the following observations:

> One of the most significant facts—arguably the most significant fact—about the universe is that we are part of it. ... Everyone agrees that the universe looks as if it was designed for life.[2]

In the 1960s, scientists had discovered 2 characteristics of the cosmos "fine-tuned" to make physical life possible and 10 characteristics of the solar system "fine-tuned" for human life to be possible. By the 2000s, scientists had discovered 38 characteristics of the cosmos recognized as "fine-tuned" for physical life and over 150 characteristics of the solar system "fine-tuned" for human life to be possible!

The slightest modifications in these 188 plus characteristics, which are delicately balanced and finely calibrated, would be disastrous for life. The delicate requirements for the existence of galaxies, star systems, and planets capable of supporting human life are incredibly fragile.

British astronomer Fred Hoyle (1915–2001), when commenting on one of these fine-tuned characteristics—the energy level needed to produce carbon in large quantities—and how statistically unlikely it was, wrote:

1 Meyer, Stephen C. *The Return of the God Hypothesis.* New York: Harper Collins Publishers, 2021. p. 108.

2 Davies, Paul. *The Goldilocks Enigma: Why is the Universe Just Right for Life?* Boston: Mariner Books, 2008, pp. 2, 191.

> Would you not say to yourself, "Some super-calculating intellect must have designed the properties of the carbon atom, otherwise the chance of my finding such an atom through the blind forces of nature would be utterly minuscule. A commonsense interpretation of the facts suggests that a super-intellect has monkeyed with physics, as well as with chemistry and biology, and that there are no blind forces worth speaking about in nature. The numbers one calculates from the facts seem to me so overwhelming as to put this conclusion almost beyond question."[3]

The most common possible explanation given by scientists from the materialist perspective is that our universe may simply be just one among a potentially infinite number of other universes—the multiverse theory—and thus was not designed. This is a theory based on absolutely no empirical evidence and thus certainly steps outside of the scientific method. Proposing an Intelligent Designer is surely far more reasonable than that!

Third, the evidence has become unquestionably strong that even the simplest forms of living things at the biochemical level contain massive amounts of digital information that is being used to produce and maintain an untold number of molecular machines and complex processes, all of which testify to design.

Antony Flew (1923–2010) was an English philosopher most notable for his work related to the philosophy of religion. He taught at the universities of Oxford, Aberdeen, Keele and Reading, and at York University in Toronto. For much of his career, Flew was known as a strong advocate of atheism, arguing that one should presuppose atheism until empirical evidence of a God surfaces. In 2003, he was one of the signatories of the Humanist Manifesto III.

Flew debated several theists including William Craig and Gary Habermas. He openly and consistently stated that his whole life had been guided by the

---

3 Hoyle, Fred. "The Universe: Past and Present Reflections." *Engineering and Science,* November 1981. pp. 8–12.

principle of Plato's Socrates: Follow the evidence, wherever it leads. In 2004 at the age of 81, he followed the evidence and explained the following in an interview with Craig Hazen and Gary Habermas:

> It has become inordinately difficult even to begin to think about constructing a naturalistic theory of the evolution of that first reproducing organism ... The enormous complexity by which the results were achieved looks to me like the work of intelligence ... It now seems to me that the finding of more than fifty years of DNA research have provided materials for a new and enormously powerful argument to design.[1]

In 2007, Dr. Flew published the book *There Is a God: How the World's Most Notorious Atheist Changed His Mind* (New York: Harper Collins Publishers, 2007).

The empirical evidence of design of living things at the biochemical level continues to grow exponentially. For our purposes here, one example from Michael Behe's latest book, Darwin Devolves, will suffice. He speaks of discoveries, mostly made since the early 2000's, of the most exquisite complexity in the building of proteins in cells.

> Subsequent work has shown that the great majority of the genes of plants and animals occur in fragments, in stretches called exons. The lengths of DNA between them are called introns. Split genes can have anywhere from one to a dozen of intron interruptions. In what order should the pieces be spliced together when introns are removed from an RNA copy of the gene? It turns out that, although they're usually stitched together in the order they are found in the DNA, sometimes one or more pieces are skipped, or duplicated, or permuted. Such "alternate splicing" uses the same gene to yield multiple proteins ... The record holder is a single gene found in the fruit fly that can yield tens of thousands of different proteins—more

1 Craig J. Hazen, Gary R. Habermas & Antony Flew, "My Pilgrimage from Atheism to Theism: An Exclusive Interview with Former British Atheist Professor Antony Flew," 2004.

> proteins than there are independent genes in the fly! ... So what equipment is needed to stitch the right pieces together with the needed exquisite accuracy?
>
> Although some bacterial introns are capable of splicing themselves, the great majority depend on a supremely complex molecular machine called the spliceosome. The spliceosome consists of a handful of dedicated RNA molecules plus hundreds of different kinds of proteins ... The spliceosome is also quite dynamic, with proteins joining and leaving it as needed as it operates.[2]

It is no wonder that historian of science, Frederic Burnham, stated in 1992 that the God hypothesis is a more respectable hypothesis today than at any time in the last 100 years.[3] In the almost thirty years since then, the evidence for a Grand Designer in these three areas of scientific research has increased exponentially.

The ancient argument from design stands on firm ground. Michael Behe said it well when he proclaimed in his seminal work:

> The result of these efforts to investigate the cell—to investigate life at the molecular level—is a loud, clear, piercing cry of *design!*[4]

Is it reasonable to believe in God in this scientific age? It is more reasonable than ever!

---

2 Behe, Michael J. *Darwin Devolves.* New York: Harper Collins Publishers, 2019, pp. 60–61

3 Cited in Briggs, David. May 2, 1992. "Science, Religion Are Discovering Commonality in Big Bang Theory." *Los Angeles Times.*

4 Behe, Michael J. *Darwin's Black Box, 10th Anniversary Edition.* New York: The Free Press, 2006, p. 232.

DR. H. E. "BUDDY" PAYNE, JR. is the Fifth President of Florida College in Temple Terrace (Tampa), Florida. Dr. Payne received his professional training at Florida College (A.A., Valedictorian), Florida State University (B.S. in Science Education, cum laude), Harvard University (M.A.T. in Science Education) and University of South Florida (Ph.D. in Mathematics Education).

He joined the Florida College faculty in 1972. He has taught chemistry and mathematics and has served as Registrar, as Dean of Students, and from 1991–2009 as Vice President and Academic Dean, guiding the College through full accreditations of its first five bachelor's degree programs.

His faith has always been of greatest importance in his life, and in 1993 he took a two-year leave of absence in order to preach the gospel in Romania following the fall of the Iron Curtain.

As a science and mathematics educator, he has devoted much time and energy to the study and discussion of intelligent design and evolution issues. He has been invited to deliver numerous lectures on this topic on college campuses and in other settings. He is also active in civic associations, including the Temple Terrace Chamber of Commerce and Tampa North Rotary Club, where he also served as president in 2002–2003.

Dr. Payne was born in 1945 in Beaumont, Texas. He and his wife Marilyn (Geer) have been married for 55 years and reside in Temple Terrace, Florida. They have four children: Valerie (Garth), Amy (Eskut), Jeannie (Chandler), Benjamin Payne, and 16 grandchildren.

Dr. Buddy Payne is Fifth President of Florida College (established 1946 as a private, non-profit liberal arts institution in Temple Terrace, Florida). He was inaugurated at Opening Ceremonies & Inauguration on Monday evening, August 24, 2009.

Lecture 10

The Church: A Place of Healing

Art Adams

What Is the Church?

This is a simple question, yet much confusion exists both in the world and in the church itself. The community concepts of "church" vary, and responses include such perceptions as: a charity, a recreation center, free entertainment and productions, ball teams and playoff competitions, food pantries, meals, schools and education centers, childcare and pre-school, singles ministries, secular support groups, a secular counseling center, and a place to learn the Bible. The answers are so varied that they are confusing. The attempts to make "church" a catch all for most anything people want to do has caused the concept of church to become little more than a social club or an elite country club where perfect people gather.

Within the church some view it as a destination, or an event as evidenced by the language "we're going to church." That is, church is a place we go to worship (a destination). Even more narrowly, some in the church see it as an educational society to teach the Bible. While this is a true partial answer, the church is to go beyond dispensing biblical truths by equipping and supporting brethren to apply the skills and messages taught. How sad that some groups teach ... teach ... teach and stop there for the most part.

We must go beyond teaching by implementing what has been taught and mentoring brethren in applying what has been taught. Judgment day is not going to be a final exam to see if we can make all the correct arguments and answer all questions like we have been taught. It will be a day to judge us on how we have applied that knowledge. Yes, we must go beyond just being a teaching society.

The word "church" means "the called out." The church is not a building or an event center. It is "the called out." We are the church! "Called out" to do what? Congregations are made up of saved people who have been called out of the world—transformed—and put back into the world to transform it by godly living, evangelism, and encouragement to each other. We are here to make a difference! Where there is no change—brethren have not answered the gospel call to "come out from among them and be separate" (2 Corinthians 6:17).

The Church Has a Mission

In business one of the first steps of organizing is answering three questions:

1. "Why do we exist?"
2. "What do we do here?"
3. "What do we not do here?"

Until these three questions are answered any organization will lack direction and focus in moving forward. The answers to these questions are germane to understanding our mission and our goals.

In the beginning, in Acts 2, the church was an exclusive organization comprised of devout Jewish people from every nation. They had come to an annual convention and while there they came to understand the reality that they had rejected their Messiah, the hope of Israel. They had offended Jehovah and were without hope having crucified their Redeemer. But then something amazing happened, three thousand were cut to their hearts crying out "what shall we do"? They were told to repent of rejecting their Lord and King and to be baptized for the remission of sins. Hmmm, "remission of sins.' This was a new concept for this crowd. Up to that time they thought of the penalty of sins being pushed forward—always owed but never paid—just postponed penalties for transgression. Their lives were about to change—forever. This was something special ... something to tell others about.

These new brethren had been called out from their way of life and transitioned into new ways of thinking. They gathered daily to study, listen, and learn. They were excited and shared. "Gladness and singleness of heart defined them." They did not get it perfectly. They were learning. Their hearts were big and their message powerful. That message moved people to change.

The start with 120 and 3,000 soon grew to 5,000 more and then we lose the numbers and see multitudes coming to be a part of their ranks.

Then, came the question: "Is the church an organization exclusive to just the Jewish people?" When the gospel moved into Samaria with a racially mixed area of Jews, perhaps some eyebrows were raised. But with Cornelius the Gentile, it took a special miracle for Peter to even enter his house. Was Peter right in baptizing a Gentile and his household? This question divided even the apostles. Peter was called back to Jerusalem to account for why he would baptize this Gentile soldier and his household. The fifteenth chapter of Acts gives an account of how this controversy was settled. Well, not totally settled. In Galatians 2:11 discrimination continued, even with an apostle. Paul withstood Peter "to the face because he stood condemned." Then, Judaizing teachers followed suit, teaching that before one could become a Christian, a member of the church, males had to first become a Jew by the physical act of circumcision.

The Gospel is For All

In the past, there have been some who tried to make the church an exclusive group by trying to eliminate some people. Taking the gospel to the whole world doesn't give the right to pick and choose who should hear the message. It is for *all*. The spirit of Diotrephes was alive then and is still active today, 3 John 9–11.

Now, back to our question: What is the church? To answer this let's look at who was invited and who answered the gospel call. Recall that the gospel was to be preached to the whole creation (Matthew 28:18–20; Mark 16:15–16). Jesus compared the message to a great dragnet that was cast and gathered all types (Matthew 13:37).

Who came?

- All who are weak and heavy laden, Matthew 11:28.
- The poor, James 2:1–12.
- Widows, Acts 6.
- The chief of sinners, 1 Timothy 1:5.

- Racially and culturally mixed, John 4; Timothy and Titus.
- The elite, John 3, Acts 9.
- Jews, Romans 1:16–17.
- Gentiles, Romans 1:21–32.
- Those sifted like wheat, Luke 22:31.
- Publicans and sinners, Luke 7:34.
- Those whose sins are many, Luke 7:36–49.
- The feebleminded and weak, 1 Thessalonians 5:14.
- Thieves, 1 Corinthians 6:11.
- Drunkards, 1 Corinthians 6:11.

What did these all have in common? They were all invited (Revelation 22:17). They were all sinners … lost … in need of a Savior. "For all have sinned and fall short of the glory of God" (Romans 3:23). "There is none righteous. No not one" (Romans 3:10–12; Psalm 14:1–3; 53:1–3). They all committed to change. Few who come into the fellowship know how to make the change. They just know that they want to change and are willing to do so. That's what repentance is. Repentance and conversion require that change. But how? It is by working as hard to teach, encourage and support them as we do to baptize them. The church's job is not to abandon dripping wet sinners at the baptistry and think our job is done.

Imperfect People

After "go … preach … baptize" is "teaching them to observe all things I have commanded you." We must move beyond wet babies to full grown mature Christians. That requires brethren and a church that spiritually supports and monitors its members as they grow. The church then is a change agent to help people transition from one way of life to a new and better way. Can we see from this that the church was not and is not made up of perfect people? Church members are in the process of growing. They are redeemed people, whose sins have been covered by the blood of Jesus. The group is composed of folks who still sin, and they grapple with their own struggles. They "confess their sins one to another" (James 5:16). Consider the passages throughout the New Testament admonishing brethren to "lay aside the sin that easily besets us" (Hebrews 12:1) and they overcome in their battle against Satan by the blood of the Lamb. To lay our sins down, confess them and ask for help, we must have a safe environment. One where all realize they have sinned and fall short ... one where we do not judge, gossip, criticize, talebear, or look down our nose with superiority.

How can this happen? When each is humble enough to see himself/herself as a sinner in need of redemption ... a sinner working on overcoming something in their own life... then we can have compassion for those asking for help by giving them a hand up and we can humbly fall down at the throne with them saying "Lord, be merciful to me a sinner." Coming into the church requires transition ... conversion ... a change. It is "a new way of life" (Ephesians 4:22–24). Members are new creatures in Christ (2 Corinthians 5:17). As with any new skills being learned, we do not expect perfection at first. Patience is needed as folks grow from milk to meat (1 Peter 2:2).

So, as we have seen, the church is composed of many types of people with a variety of life experiences. The church, then, is not a country club for perfect people. It is much like a hospital for sick and healing folks. What is the environment the saved can provide to welcome and nurture new converts and to provide security for those who may be struggling?

The Church Is Like a Hospital

Any successful organization must have and understand its mission. This is core. When a facility begins to dwindle, leaders must go back to basics – what is our mission? A mission statement needs to be exclusive and answer some questions: what do we do? and what do we not do? So, what is the mission of the church? Answer: To seek and save the lost through evangelism, edification of the members and to assist our members with benevolence as needed, Matthew 28:18-20; Ephesians 4:14-16; 1 Corinthians 16:1-2. Memorize this. It is core. Everything we do must fall with these boundaries or else, we do not do it.

Like a hospital, a local church must understand the scope of its services, which is:

1. To spread the gospel to our community and to the world.

2. To assist our members in spiritual grow and development of their talents.

This next function provides specific targets. Long and short term goals which are measurable need to be established. This answers the question "what are we trying to accomplish?" Long term goals are usually 3–, 5–, or 10–year goals. Where do we want this congregation to be in these intervals? These need to be specific and measurable, like double in size in 5 years. Short term goals address what we want to accomplish in the next 3, 6, 9, or 12 months and align with our long-term goals.

Our guiding principle is:

All have sinned. All are sick, lost and dying.
The world is in a pandemic; we, the church,
deploy and help folks recover.

Like a hospital, there are some administrative functions to the church. The head of this organization is Jesus (Ephesians 1:22–23). In the startup phase, apostles and prophets helped lay the framework (Ephesians 2:20). The foundation being laid, we build on it (as living stones). Now in Ephesians 4, Paul addresses the gifts. "He gave some to be apostles, some prophets and some… Pastors. Pastors (shepherds, elders, presbyters, overseers) is a plural term denoting those with administrative spiritual oversight of the congregation. The congregation is to follow their lead and obey their oversight (Hebrews 13:7, 17).

Evangelists are heralds or mouthpieces with the primary responsibility of preaching the word—sounding out the message. This is not an idle position but spoken of as "the work of an evangelist" (2 Timothy 4:5). This involves finding people who will listen. The last gift listed is teachers. Now, is this list short a few spots, like deacons and members? I think not. Teachers—is a term inclusive of every Christian. Every member is responsible for evangelism. There is no position or gift of pew warmer or financial backer. There is work for all in these "gifts" of Ephesians 4. In Acts 6, the seven men appointed to distribute money did more than that. Consider one of the seven, Stephen, preaching to the Sanhedrin, and Phillip the evangelist, who taught and baptized an Ethiopian. These were two of the seven servants (deacons) of Acts 6. Yes, they were teachers. Or, consider Acts 8, where those scattered abroad "went everywhere preaching the gospel". Everyone was involved in ministering to the lost—that is—teaching. All of us are in this list in Ephesians 4. Are we filling our roles to make the church ready to welcome newcomers and help one another?

A hospital may have a beautiful facility and an outstandingly qualified administrative team and still fail. Why? The Marketing or Outreach function must be in place, targeted and having successful outcomes to fill beds. In Luke 14:23 Jesus addressed marketing "the highways, byways, hedges ... that my house may be filled." We must reach the ones we are trying to help—the sick and dying—the lost. Otherwise, we just have a nice building and a top-notch administrative team.

A hospital, likewise, must have a treatment team. These are persons skilled in varying approaches to quality care. A spiritual treatment team may simply sit with the patients, minister to their needs, operate to bring about spiritual health or provide radical treatment. Treatment teams help tend to those who are contagious. Galatians 6:1 describes going into a danger zone to help a member, "considering yourself lest you be tempted."

Unfortunately, hospitals have a morgue. Some are overcome by their disease (in this case, sin). Some shall depart from the faith (1 Timothy 4:1). It is sad when one has known the way of truth, led others to know Jesus and then turns away. As sad as it is, not everyone we try to help will survive. We cannot afford to let that discourage us. We must move on to help those who respond to our help. When a patient is appreciative of what has been done for them, he or she needs to be eager to return the favor and pass the blessing on to others. Paul talked about lighting the torch in someone else's hands: "the words I have committed to you, the same pass on to others" (2 Timothy 12:2).

Now which part of the hospital and services are most important? All are. Without leadership a hospital will fail. Without a treatment team there is no one to provide services. Without patients there is no one to care for. All are important and necessary. Is this not Paul's message in 1 Corinthians 12:16, 17? Are we ready to receive sinners seeking a Savior? Does this church welcome sinners? All sinners?

Conclusion

Why is the church not growing like it once did? Some are quick to say, "People just aren't interested." Really? The CBD oil industry has grown at a steep spike and made millionaires of many during the pandemic. They grew with persistence. Alcoholics Anonymous, Alanon, Sex Addicts Anonymous, Sanon, Celebrate Recovery, and ball teams are flourishing. People go to great lengths to attend and participate in these. Mental Health and Addictions facilities are at capacity with up to 2 month waiting lists. Jesus said the problem is not the seed (the word of God). The problem ... the real problem ... is "the laborers are few". The seed is still in the barn. Growth is in direct proportion to what is being sown.

Forgetting our purpose and mission we may try to compete with other religious groups. Suppose I drove up to the ER entrance, jumped out of my car and the attendants came running out with a gurney. Then, I say to them "change my oil and filter and rotate my tires." Their startled reply might be, "we don't do that here." Suppose I say, "Well why not? Are you anti tire rotation and oil change?" They might say, "No, that's not our mission. Our mission is to help sick people." That's our mission, too.

We seek and save the lost.

Jesus did not die on the cross so we can have potlucks, ball teams, games and frolic. Let's do that somewhere else and stay true to our mission. See the church as a hospital to help sick people and stay in focus. Yes, we are not a group for perfect people, but a hospital for sick people. Come and meet our Chief of Staff. He is the Great Physician. He can heal your life, too.

ART ADAMS currently serves as the CEO for Emerald Neuro Recover in Carmel, IN and specializes in delivering clinical mental health and addiction services to patients. He also serves as the executive director for Leaving the Pit Behind in Indianapolis. Leaving the Pit Behind provides addiction and clinical services and consultation to faith-based organizations. He has conducted national seminars and clinical retreats on parenting; substance dependence; anger; dealing with difficult people; pornography; betrayed women; anxiety; depression; conflict resolution; home and family; and more. Art has preached for congregations in Portage, IN; Oglethorpe, GA; Gary, IN; and currently in Plymouth, IN.

Lecture 11

Christians and Higher Education

Shane Scott

Consider these three statistics:

1. Over two-thirds of American high school students will go on to college.
2. Two-thirds of American young adults who regularly attended church in high school stop attending for at least a year between the ages of 18–22.
3. Of those who stop attending, almost half say attending college played a major role in the decision.[1]

Taken together, these numbers reveal what many of us have witnessed firsthand—young disciples who pursue higher education often make shipwreck of their faith.

Why?

One factor is the nature of higher education itself. Scripture warns about the dangers of human wisdom disconnected from the fear of the Lord.

> See to it that no one takes you captive by philosophy and empty deceit, according to human tradition, according to the elemental spirits of the world, and not according to Christ (Colossians 2:8 ESV).

To the extent that higher education tempts students to abandon submission to God's authority and create their own path, it mimics the strategy of the serpent in Genesis 3 who enticed Adam and Eve to ignore the will of God and follow their own will. Instead of being a place where the student gives the teacher an apple, school becomes the place where the teacher offers the student the forbidden fruit of human autonomy.

---

1 Stats are from https://admissionsly.com/percentage-who-go-to-college and https://baptistcourier.com/2019/02/study-confirms-majority-of-college-students-drop-out-of-church/.

Another factor is the nature of going away to college, leaving behind the constant oversight of parents. College is usually the first time in a young person's life when they get to experience regularly waking up on their own, getting fed on their own, and going to worship on their own. And unless their college has rules in place, it is often the first time a young disciple can freely choose how to live without parental supervision. It is all too easy to use this freedom as "an opportunity for the flesh" (Galatians 5:13).

I'm not suggesting that knowledge only puffs up college students, or that lukewarmness and licentiousness are unique temptations for students that age. These issues face disciples of all ages. But young disciples typically face these challenges for the very first time on their own once they enter college.

The Bible does not specifically address the issue of higher education and the particular challenges it presents to young Christians, but it does contain principles that we can apply to this exciting but dangerous time in life. And there is at least one story of young people of God who go far away from home to be educated (against their will—not unlike some kids I know!). That's the story of Daniel and his friends. So, I want to use that account, along with guidance drawn from other passages, to strengthen young disciples as they enter higher education.

The Story of Daniel

Let's begin our look at the story of Daniel with a little historical background. The last years of the kingdom of Judah were marked by political vacillation, as the leaders of the nation had to decide how to deal with the growing threat of Babylon. Some leaders chose a pro-Babylonian policy, while others tried to stand up to Babylon (spurred on by promises of Egyptian assistance, which never came). The last of the righteous kings of Judah, Josiah, refused an alliance with Egypt, and actually went to war with Pharaoh Neco, losing his life in the process. The Egyptians retaliated by removing Josiah's son—Jehoahaz—from the throne, replacing him with a king of their choosing, his brother, Eliakim, whom he renamed Jehoiakim. This did not sit well with Egypt's rival to the north, Babylon, and in 605 BC its new king, Nebuchadnezzar, marched on Jerusalem. As 2 Kings 24:1 records: "In his days, Nebuchadnezzar king of Babylon came up, and Jehoiakim became his servant three years."

This is where the story of Daniel begins:

> In the third year of the reign of Jehoiakim king of Judah, Nebuchadnezzar king of Babylon came to Jerusalem and besieged it. And the Lord gave Jehoiakim king of Judah into his hand, with some of the vessels of the house of God. And he brought them to the land of Shinar, to the house of his god, and placed the vessels in the treasury of his god. Then the king commanded Ashpenaz, his chief eunuch, to bring some of the people of Israel, both of the royal family and of the nobility, youths without blemish, of good appearance and skillful in all wisdom, endowed with knowledge, understanding learning, and competent to stand in the king's palace, and to teach them the literature and language of the Chaldeans. The king assigned them a daily portion of the food that the king ate, and of the wine that he drank. They were to be educated for three years, and at the end of that time they were to stand before the king. Among these were Daniel, Hananiah, Mishael, and Azariah of the tribe of Judah. And the chief of the eunuchs gave them names: Daniel he called Belteshazzar, Hananiah he called Shadrach, Mishael he called Meshach, and Azariah he called Abednego (Daniel 1:1–7).

Nebuchadnezzar gave orders to take some of the royal family and nobility for two reasons. On the one hand these young men essentially became hostages, giving the Babylonians leverage in case Judah rebelled again. And on the other hand, these boys would be useful tools for diplomacy.

The fact that Ashpenaz, the "chief eunuch" (1:3) was given charge may imply the boys were to become eunuchs, as Isaiah prophesied. They were to be the cream of the crop in every way according to verse 4. To prepare them for their future role as government officials, they were immersed in Babylonian culture (1:4–7) including a new language, a new diet, and new names.

Since naming something or someone is an act of authority, it was common practice in the ancient world to re-name a foreigner under your sovereignty (Joseph became Zaphenath-panea, Genesis 41:45; Haddasah became Esther, Esther 2:7). Just as many Hebrew names contain the name of God (*El* for *Elohim,* or *iah* for LORD), the new names given by the Babylonians reflect their many gods:

- Daniel (God is my Judge)—Belteshazzar (Lady of Bel protect the king).
- Hananiah (LORD is gracious)—Shadrach (fearful of God or command of Aku).
- Mishael (Who is what God is?)—Meshach (I am of little account or who is like Aku?).
- Azariah (LORD is a helper)—Abednego (servant of Nebo).

Imagine being a thousand miles away from home, immersed in a completely foreign culture. As exiles in a climate that is hostile to their convictions, how could Daniel and his three friends maintain their commitment to God? This is the same question facing all of us, isn't it? We, like Daniel and his friends, are also in exile.

> Beloved, I urge you as sojourners and exiles to abstain from the passions of the flesh, which wage war against your soul (1 Peter 2:11).

All of us are Christians living in the world but not of it. All of us can learn from Daniel's faith. But since he and his friends were young, Daniel's story is especially appropriate for college students. Let's see how these young "strangers and exiles" handled their new station in life.

All Truth Is God's Truth

Daniel and his friends were taught the "literature and language" of the Babylonians for three years (1:4–5). What could these Jewish youths possibly learn of importance from their new Babylonian overlords? What could pagans teach those who confess that the LORD God is one (Deuteronomy 6:4)?

I once heard someone say that "all truth is God's truth." I wish I could remember who it was because I would like to thank them for a helpful reminder that has stayed with me through many years of education. Since God is the creator, all of reality (and all knowledge of it) ultimately comes from God. All truth is God's truth!

This is the reason that the wise man can point to the behavior of ants and expect the sluggard to learn something from it, Proverbs 6:6–11. Because God made the ants and the natural order in which they live, the truth that can be gleaned from the ants is from God. But in this case, it is not truth that is delivered in tablets of stone from the top of a mountain, but truth that is observed from the ground up—literally. This is also why there are sections of Proverbs 22:17–24:34, that resemble ancient wisdom sayings from Egypt.[1] Since truths like the work habits of the ant are inherent to the natural order that God made, these truths are accessible to everyone. Therefore, if wise men in Egypt—or Babylon—truly uncovered that which is true in their observations of the creation, it would ultimately be to the Creator's credit. All truth is God's truth!

This means that when we study the natural sciences, we are really studying the work of God. The processes we observe on a regular basis, such as the water cycle, photosynthesis, or the food chain, are in fact God's regular providential care for His creation, watering the mountains from His watery abode (Psalm 104:13); causing the grass to grow (Psalm 104:14); and giving the young lions their prey (Psalm 104:21). It is when the natural sciences repudiate the knowledge of God and assume that the natural order is the result of blind chance that it ceases to be science and becomes dogma. But because as Christians we understand that there could be no "natural" process, and no nature at all, without God, we gladly confess, "O LORD, how manifold are your works!" as we study the natural sciences (Psalm 104:24).

Further, the truth that is revealed from the top down—the Scripture—was written in a historical context and a literary form. A good education in history, literature, and grammar can be a tremendous help in studying the

1 *The Instruction of Amenemopet.*

Scriptures, just as logic and philosophy can sharpen the critical thinking skills needed to analyze the meaning of a text. But in all cases, the value of such an education is a means to the end of glorifying God, not the end in and of itself. Isolated from God, education becomes a dead end, just as any other human endeavor does when it ignores God (see Ecclesiastes 2 for many examples).

Daniel and his friends took what they learned in their years of study with the Babylonians and used it for God's glory. "God gave them learning and skill in all literature and wisdom" (Daniel 1:17). That is what all students should do with the education they receive. The early church writer Augustine described the proper use of a pagan education like this:

> For, as the Egyptians had not only the idols and heavy burdens which the people of Israel hated and fled from, but also vessels and ornaments of gold and silver, and garments, which the same people when going out of Egypt appropriated to themselves, designing them for a better use, not doing this on their own authority, but by the command of God, the Egyptians themselves, in their ignorance, providing them with things which they themselves were not making a good use of; in the same way all branches of heathen learning have not only false and superstitious fancies and heavy burdens of unnecessary toil, which every one of us, when going out under the leadership of Christ from the fellowship of the heathen, ought to abhor and avoid; but they contain also liberal instruction which is better adapted to the use of the truth, and some most excellent precepts of morality; and some truths in regard even to the worship of the One God are found among them. Now these are, so to speak, their gold and silver, which they did not create themselves, but dug out of the mines of God's providence which are everywhere scattered abroad, and are perversely and unlawfully prostituting to the worship of devils. These, therefore, the Christian, when he separates himself in spirit from the miserable fellowship of these men, ought to take away from them, and to devote to their proper use in preaching the gospel.[2]

2 *On Christian Doctrine,* Book II.40.60.

"Liberal instruction" (as Augustine described it) is not a bad thing. It is "liberal" in the sense of that which gives liberty, freedom from slavery to mere instinct or turbulent passion to be what makes us fully human (the capacities to know, do, and love). In our culture, education once focused on the True, Good, and Beautiful, which in the final analysis come from God. As Plato put it, "The power to learn is present in everyone's soul ... turning the whole soul until it is able to study that which is and the brightest thing that is, namely, the one we call the good."[1] The early history of higher education in our country was explicitly religious (the original motto of Harvard was *Christo et Ecclesiae,* "For Christ and the Church"). Obviously, our secular age no longer believes education is focused on God, but every Christian can still focus on education in a God-centered way, so long as he or she remembers that all truth is God's truth, and education, like everything we do, is "for the glory of God" (1 Corinthians 10:31).

But there is another factor that makes higher education a challenge to young Christians. And we can also learn how to deal with it from Daniel and his friends.

Abstain from Fleshly Lusts

The issue of purity also confronted Daniel and his friends as they were immersed in their new culture.

> But Daniel resolved that he would not defile himself with the king's food, or with the wine that he drank. Therefore he asked the chief of the eunuchs to allow him not to defile himself (Daniel 1:8).

Daniel did not want to eat the royal diet because he believed it would defile him. Why did he fear this? Part of the reason may be the kosher laws in Leviticus 11. Since the Law gave a strict guideline for what could be eaten, Daniel may have felt the safest course in a strange country may have been to avoid everything but vegetables and water. This doesn't seem to fully explain why Daniel did not want to drink the wine, which was allowed under the Law, but it may have been a big factor in his concern.

1 *The Republic,* Book VII.

Another issue to keep in mind is the connection in the ancient world between food and idolatry. Even in the NT period Paul had to warn the Corinthians about eating in pagan temples. Perhaps Daniel thought that the meat and wine would have been part of pagan sacrifices, and he did not want to be defiled with eating something used in idolatrous worship.

And it may have just been that Daniel wanted to reserve one part of his life from Babylonian influence so that he would not become completely identified as a pagan. He spoke their language, learned in their schools, bore their name. At least he could draw the line at what he ate.

Whatever the specific issues were in Daniel's mind, he was convicted about the need for purity, and God blessed him as a result.

> And God gave Daniel favor and compassion in the sight of the chief of the eunuchs, and the chief of the eunuchs said to Daniel, "I fear my lord the king, who assigned your food and your drink; for why should he see that you were in worse condition than the youths who are of your own age? So you would endanger my head with the king." Then Daniel said to the steward whom the chief of the eunuchs had assigned over Daniel, Hananiah, Mishael, and Azariah, "Test your servants for ten days; let us be given vegetables to eat and water to drink. Then let our appearance and the appearance of the youths who eat the king's food be observed by you, and deal with your servants according to what you see." So he listened to them in this matter, and tested them for ten days. At the end of ten days it was seen that they were better in appearance and fatter in flesh than all the youths who ate the king's food. So the steward took away their food and the wine they were to drink, and gave them vegetables (Daniel 1:9–16).

Daniel knew there was a war for his soul, that he needed to take drastic measures to make sure he did not defile himself. And with God's help, he and his friends maintained their integrity.

Now, I am not promising that if you keep yourself pure in your personal life that you will be the top of your class (though I did become "fatter in flesh" by eating too much pizza in college!). But what I am saying is that if Daniel and his friends could maintain their faith commitment so far from home, without parents or spiritual guardians, then it is possible for young disciples to "abstain from fleshly lusts" as Peter would put it. In the next chapter of the book, Daniel prays: "To you, O God of my fathers, I give thanks and praise, for you have given me wisdom and might" (Daniel 2:23a). The reason Daniel kept his convictions is because they were his convictions. His faith was his faith. He loved God, and just because his zip code changed (if they had zip codes in the ancient world!), his faith did not.

It may be the case that the statistics which show young people losing their faith in college are just exposing the lack of faith those students had in high school. And to the extent this is so, it is imperative that young disciples begin drawing closer to God right now. Faith is like a spiritual investment. Some young people take what's given to them and bury it in a hole like the one talent man, leaving it behind when they go to school. But wise young disciples take the spiritual investment given to them and compound it into their own faith. They will enter into the joy of their Master.

It is very tough to be a Christian, to be an exile. The transition to adulthood that occurs during the college years is a crucial milestone in the journey of exiles. But it is also exciting, and when pursued to the glory of God and in purity of heart, it is one of the happiest stages of the journey home. "For here we have no lasting city, but we seek the city that is to come" (Hebrews 13:14).

SHANE SCOTT was born and raised in Winchester, KY. He attended Florida College from 1985–1989, earning the four-year Bible diploma. After graduating, he began preaching in central Kentucky, and since then his local work has taken him to Chicagoland and to Nashville. Currently, he preaches in the Tampa, FL area for the Valrico congregation. Shane was also on the Biblical Studies faculty at Florida College for three years. Shane was married to Kristi (Bennett) for seven years before her passing in 2018. In his spare time, Shane is an avid Kentucky Wildcats fan, and also sings in a barbershop quartet.

Lecture 12

Interacting with Other Faiths

Andrew Roberts

A century ago, evangelism in the U.S. concerned correcting and countering aberrant forms of Christianity. The plea was, "Restore—take the Bible as the authority in Faith and Practice." Evangelism meant demonstrating "the way of God more accurately" to gospel-leaning people and exhorting them to leave denominationalism or Catholicism.

That approach was good for reaching our neighbors. It recognized where they were, spiritually speaking. Now, though, religion in American communities is arguably the most diverse it has been since the founding of the United States. Many of our neighbors are not church members.[1]

Americans hold to other faiths: world religions, cults, and (in ever increasing numbers) to no religion at all. There are as many Muslims in the United States as Methodists. The American Buddhist population is estimated at 3-4 million. Pew Research Center found that Hinduism holds the highest retention rate—80% of Americans raised Hindu remain throughout adulthood. The Church of Scientology has its own television channel. Mormons and Jehovah's Witnesses canvas neighborhoods knocking doors. Our neighbors entertain any of these faith systems or invent their own.[2]

---

1 From 1937–1997 approximately 70% of Americans self-identified as Church Members. This level of participation in Churches has steeply declined over the past 25 years. In 2020, only 47% of Americans said they belonged to a Church, synagogue or Mosque. See Jeffrey M. Jones, "U.S. Church Membership Falls Below Majority for First Time" Gallup (https://news.gallup.com/poll/341963/church-membership-falls-below-majority-first-time.aspx, March 29, 2021).

2 I recently invited a gas station attendant to worship with me at church on Sunday. She laughed out-loud in my face. She could see my feelings were hurt at her reaction and explained to me that she goes to church in the woods. When she is in the woods, all by herself, that is her church. She told me that her husband goes to church on his boat. When he is out on the ocean, looking up at the sky, he is in church. She assured me that on Sunday they'd either be on the water or in the woods. Obviously, they are other-faith people, but their faith seems to be entirely of their own making.

Then there is "None"-Faith, which has dramatically risen over the past 25 years. Younger Americans seem less likely to commit to any religion. 36% of millennials[3] in the United States are religious "Nones," that is, people unaffiliated with any type of faith at all.[4] Gen Z follows them closely.[5] One-third of all Americans consider themselves non-religious, saying, "religion is not an important part of their daily life and that they seldom or never attend religious services."[6] Indeed, if all non-religious people formed a single religion, it would be the world's third largest.

1. Christianity (2.3 billion adherents).
2. Islam (1.8 billion adherents).
3. Non-religious—Secular/Agnostic/Atheist (1.2 billion adherents).
4. Hinduism (1.1 billion adherents).[7]

Christians, this couldn't be a more exciting time! These religious shifts situate us on the original trail Christians blazed when they went everywhere preaching the word (Acts 8:4). Interacting with other faiths was the gospel mission two thousand years ago and it is evangelism in twenty-first century America.

---

3 Millennials is a sociological label for the generation of Americans born between 1980–1995.

4 Pew Research Center, "America's Changing Religious Landscape," (pewforum.org, May 12, 2015) 18–29.

5 Emerging data on Gen Z (teenagers/ twenty-somethings) complements the millennials. Eight out of ten report they believe "in God or a universal spirit." They are drawn to an amorphous deism seeking expression and community without defined religions. For these youths, social justice work is taking on a Faith dimension for "being part of something that is transcending, that is bigger than oneself." See Maya Jaradat, "Gen Z's looking for religion. You'd be surprised where they find it" *Deseret News* (https://www.deseret.com/indepth/2020/9/13/21428404/gen-z-religion-spirituality-social-justice-black-lives-matter-parents-family-pandemic, Sep 13, 2020).

6 Frank Newport, "In U.S., Four in 10 Report Attending Church in Last Week," Gallup (gallup.com/poll December 24, 2013)

7 Conrad Hackett and David McClendon, "Christians Remain World's Largest Religious Group, But They Are Declining In Europe" *Pew Research Center* (pewresearch.org, April 5, 2017); See also Gabe Bullard, "The World's Newest Major Religion: No Religion," *National Geographic* (news.nationalgeographic.com, April 22, 2016)

The Great Commission did not bring religion to a world without religion (Matthew 28:18–20). On the contrary, nearly everyone in the world had some religious adherence. In fact, Antiquity even had skeptics like Epicurus who doubted if there even was a God (or gods).[1]

Right away Christians were interacting with other faiths. They answered falsehoods promoted against them (Matthew 5:10–12). For instance, Judean authorities called Christians, "blasphemers" (Acts 6:11–14). The way was falsely labeled a "sect" (Acts 24:14–15). As Christianity spread to Gentile regions, Christians were accused of turning the world upside down and slandered as rebels for confessing Jesus as king (Acts 17:6–7).[2]

But through it all the Christians persisted. The message of the cross of Christ gained traction and people stepped out of their culture and religion at great personal cost to follow Jesus Christ (Matthew 10:32–39).

Disciples of Jesus set themselves apart, not for offering another religion, but for telling the truth (John 14:6; 17:17; Colossians. 1:5). They were famous—maybe infamous—for courage and their willingness to suffer for their convictions (1 Thessalonians 1:6–10; Revelation 2:8–11; 13).

Suffer they did. Civics and religion were intertwined to undergird the fabric of Roman society. The Way threatened to unwind it by labeling all the gods (with their idols, temples, priesthoods, festivals, economies) false and immoral (Acts 19:23–27). So, the vocal minority of Christians suffered persecution.

---

1 Epicurus' (341–270 BC) skepticism was due in part to the quandary of evil in the world. He reasoned, "Either God wants to abolish evil, and cannot; or he can, but does not want to; or he cannot and does not want to. If he wants to, but cannot, he is impotent. If he can, and does not want to, he is wicked. But, if God both can and wants to abolish evil, then how come evil is in the world?"

2 In the second and third centuries Christians were called atheists because they did not believe in the Roman gods and refused to burn incense to them. Saints were maligned as cannibals rumored to eat flesh and drink blood. See Minucius Felix, Octavius, (https://sourcebooks.fordham.edu/ancient/christian-cannibals.asp)

If our society continues to religiously diversify where will that leave us? Maligned, misunderstood, even a minority Faith? That's where Christianity started (1 Corinthians 1:20, 26; 1 Peter 4:12; 2 Timothy 1:8–12; 3:12).

What's needed is the boldness and zeal of the first century church. Interacting with other faiths requires a shift in attitude. Let's LOVE our neighbors. Let's LOVE people of other faiths. That's how we interact with them in the gospel: LOVE.

L—Love the Lord and Your Neighbors

There are two essential behaviors to making disciples of Christ. If Christians do these two things, then more people will be added to Christ's Kingdom through the gospel.

1. Make personal connections. We must meet people. We are socialized not to talk to strangers, but the Great Commission directs us to do that very thing. Evangelism does not happen if we do not make personal connections.[3]
2. Have spiritual conversations. It is our responsibility to initiate spiritual/religious talk with others. This is how we find people interested in spiritual things. We want to present the gospel at least once.[4]

If your congregation is doing those two things, you'll start interacting with other faiths quickly.

Love is essential. Love casts out fear about interacting with other faiths (1 John 4:18). We love because Jesus first loved us (1 John 4:19). We love what He loves and He loves the world (John 3:16). He does not love sin,

---

3 Not every Christian is an extrovert. We all have different functions in the body of Christ. That said, if all your associations are saints your influence is too limited. It is time to interact with people who are not Christians so they experience your salt and light, Matthew 5:13–16.

4 For a gospel presentation with "None-Faith" people in mind which easily leads to more in-depth Bible studies, see: www.ineedgoodnewstoday.com . Not every Christian is a Teacher. However we can connect people with teachers and we can forward links to our neighbors with gospel content.

pride, idolatry, or false religions. But He loves the people of the world. He died to free them from their sins. He offers the Truth and calls them to repentance (John 8:31–32; Luke 24:46–47).

Let the truth of God's love be seen in us. Love practices the Golden Rule, treating people the way we desire to be treated (Matthew 7:12). You desire to be heard and respected as a person. You desire courtesy even if people disagree. You desire people to take you at your word and not mock, slander, or ascribe the worst motives to your words and deeds. That's how we need to treat people of other faiths.

Love is the Greatest Commandment—Love God above all and love your neighbor as yourself (Matthew 22:36–40). Seek the good of your neighbor because he is your neighbor—made in the image of God. Your ability to help, bless, and encourage is not dependent upon sharing faith with that neighbor. Of course, there are blessings of fellowship for the family of God in the local church. But as an individual, the Greatest Commandment is toward your neighbor. When you show mercy to the needful around you then you are a neighbor to them. One day they will die and meet the Lord in Judgment. You have not loved a neighbor if you never mentioned the gospel—this is the mercy they require above all else.

The truth is to be spoken in love (Ephesians 4:15). Love is the motivation that reaches souls with truth. Sometimes truth is called "hate" and Christians are called "hateful" for believing it or repeating God's Word on a subject. But there is nothing unloving about showing someone the truth. The unloving thing is to hide it and allow people to live and die without it.

Love people because Jesus does. Love does not mean approving of sin or false religion. Jesus does not approve of sin. But you are as peaceable, merciful, gracious, and helpful (in so far as you can help) to people of other faiths because that's how Jesus loves us. Love impresses people because no other religion has anything comparable to the love of Christ.

O—Observe Your Neighbor's Religion

Thanks to the internet (especially YouTube and Facebook), it is easier than ever to educate yourself about another religion. In 2018 only 10% of churches in the United States were streaming services online. By 2021 only 10% of churches in the United States were *not* streaming services online.[1] It wasn't just churches. Religious groups of all faiths and sizes in the U.S. went online due to the pandemic.

You can easily sneak-a-peak at a livestream worship or online teaching to observe another religion. Take it one neighbor at a time. Invest the effort to watch a few videos or do a Google search for the basic tenants and history of their religion. This allows you to arrive at some educated guesses at what presuppositions your other-faith neighbor holds. Furthermore, it will generate some spiritual questions in your mind about their beliefs.

Such observation affords you a basic vocabulary for more meaningful conversation and study. It will help you to know what you do not know about their Faith. Those are the things which you can use to drive spiritual conversations. Think of it as a demonstration of sincerity and respect. Your effort to learn something about a subject before passing judgment upon it is usually appreciated.

Remember this is a two-way street. Your other-faith neighbor is observing Christianity from what he sees online or television. Do not fail to apprise yourself of the teachings and views of big-media "Church" personalities. "None"–Faith people (Millennials, Gen Z) are huge media consumers. So, part of interacting with other faiths is thinking through responses when your other-faith friend says, "I was watching Joyce Meyer the other night and she said..." or "Is your preacher like Joel Osteen? He's great!" How will you capitalize on that media exposure?

V—Verify Your Neighbor's Beliefs

"None"-Faith is not anti-faith. The Millennials and Gen Z want to blend their own eclectic spiritual tastes into a personal faith—a hyper-individualization

1 Carey Nieuwhof Leadership Podcast (https://careynieuwhof.com/episode382/).

of religion. Even adherents of established religions admit they disagree with or reject particular tenants/teachings. A popular view is, "Nobody believes everything in their religion. You find the one that works best for you."

Learn to verify your neighbor's beliefs. Not all self-professed Christians believe and practice alike. We understand there's a host of reasons for it. Likewise, variations exist within world religions. Even greater diversity can be expected among people who are literally feeling their own personal religion as they go along. So, ask spiritual questions. Verify—do not assume.

Consider these questions for any religion or philosophy. Where is your other-faith neighbor on these?

- Where did we come from?
- Why are we here?
- Why is the world the way that it is—broken with evil, pain, and suffering?
- What is to be done about it?
- What happens next—when we die? What is the future of the world?

Every religion or philosophy attempts to satisfy these questions. People decide which answers to believe and orient their understanding of the world. God's Word answers all of these questions and those answers accord with reality.

There's a give and take in spiritual conversations. People of other faiths want to tell you about their religion. That bit of observation you did about your neighbor's religion pays off when you can ask something specific, even tailor the questions listed above to their religion. Furthermore, they will probably ask you questions about Christianity.

I love the night I met a young Muslim man on a university campus who began his question by saying, "Tell me truly, Christian ..." He had always wanted to ask a Christian a few things and there I was—"the Christian." In those golden moments, do your best to answer with God's Word, the Bible.

That night I had a Bible with me, and I said, "I will show you in the Bible what it says. We will read it. And what it says is what I believe about the question." The more often you call the Bible, "God's Word," the better.

Your willingness to verify their faith by asking questions shows that you are passionate about spiritual things. You could mention, "I'm a person of faith, it's important to me. That's why I asked. You seem like a person of faith too." But as the conversation continues, make clear that, "I am interested in truth." Faith is quite subjective, but truth is objective. Plenty of people sincerely believe untruths. My goal is to know the truth and believe what is true. My goal is to persuade others to believe what is true.

There is power in answering the spiritual questions we are asked with God's Word—Book, Chapter, and Verse—because it is the truth (John 17:17; Hebrews 4:12). Bibles are ubiquitous on smart phones. The more we can answer spiritual questions with the Bible and drive people to read the Bible with us—or even on their own—the more they see the truth. God's Word prompts a shift in thinking from *My* Faith to *The* Truth (John 8:31–32).

E—Entreat the Lord

Matthew 9:35–38 describes Jesus' travels to villages preaching the gospel of the Kingdom. He was compassionate toward the people. He told His disciples, "The harvest truly is plentiful, but the laborers are few. Therefore pray the Lord of the harvest to send out laborers into His harvest." The Lord's church is the answer to this prayer. Will you entreat the Lord for evangelistic efforts in your congregation?

Interacting with other faiths quickly drives Christians to prayer. If you are in a prayer-rut, initiate some evangelistic action. You'll be praying like crazy when you start reading the Bible with a Muslim friend, door-knocking in a Hindu neighborhood, or organizing a MeetUp for the spiritually curious or skeptical.[1]

---

1 MeetUp.com.

The first Christians were all interacting with other faiths. Notice they entreated the Lord for:

- Boldness and courage to continue (Acts 4:29-31; Ephesians 6:20).
- Open doors—opportunity and time (Ephesians 6:19; Colossians 4:2–3).
- Wisdom (Colossians 4:5–6; James 1:5).
- Proper speech (Colossians 4:6).
- Fruitfulness and blessing upon the preaching (1 Corinthians 3:5–7; 1 Thessalonians 5:2–10.

The urgent outcry of fervent prayer is ignited over specific names and situations when we are interacting with other faiths. Pray and continue to pray.

Conclusion

Initially it is intimidating to talk about the gospel with someone from a different religious background – some other faith. But those are the people who are around us. This is our time to be Christ's kingdom on earth and do our part in the Great Commission. As we LOVE these people, we soon discover the excitement and privilege of making disciples by the gospel of Jesus Christ. Going into the world starts with our neighbors—*Interacting with Other Faiths.*

For Further Reading

Ryan P. Burge, *The Nones: Where They Came From, Who They Are, and Where They Are Going* (Fortress Press, 2021).

Monte Cox, *Significant Others: Understanding Our Non-Christian Neighbors* (Leafwood Press, 2017).

Elizabeth Drescher, *Choosing Our Religion: The Spiritual Lives of America's Nones* (Oxford University Press, 2016).

Gregory Koukl, *Tactics: A Game Plan for Discussing Your Christian Convictions,* Updated & Expanded (Zondervan, 2019).

Mike Willis, ed., *Refocusing on Evangelism: An Examination of Evangelism in the 21st Century* (Truth Books, 2015).

ANDREW ROBERTS is privileged to serve as a minister and evangelist among churches of Christ. His joy for communicating Bible truths has encouraged people for nearly twenty years. Andrew has accepted invitations to speak at lectureships and conferences in churches, schools, universities, and businesses from Alaska to Florida. His articles have appeared in *Truth Magazine, Biblical Insights,* and *Pressing On* e-magazine. He lives with his wife, Julie, and three children in Tampa, FL. His Spiritbuilding titles include *Night and Day: A Comparative Study of Christianity and Islam; The Purity Pursuit; The Gospel and You;* and *The Lion Is the Lamb: The King of Kings, His Glorious Kingdom, and His Promised Return.*

Lecture 13

Judges or Messengers?

Don Truex

His words were simple, the implications profound: "I did not come to judge the world but to save the world. The one who rejects me and does not receive My words, has a judge; the word that I have spoken will judge him on the last day" (John 12:47–48). There is a beautiful symmetry in that passage, "not to judge ... but to save."

There is, however, an ugly abuse often made of that passage, e.g., a smokescreen for impenitence or a tolerance of behavior that God would certainly find intolerable. Jesus, of course, judged many individuals, most notably the Pharisees (cf. Matthew 23). And He commissioned us to do the same regarding the character traits required of shepherds (1 Timothy 3), Christians "overtaken in a fault" (Galatians 6:1), and brethren who are to be avoided because they "cause divisions and offenses" (Romans 16:17).

Nevertheless, the words are plain, "I did not come to judge." Perhaps He had in mind the harsh, calloused, censorious judgment of Matthew 7:1. After all, Jesus dealt fairly, righteously with friends and enemies alike. Or perhaps it was an affirmation of His words in John 3:17, i.e., "God did not send His Son into the world to condemn the world, but in order that the world might be saved through Him." After all, the world was already judged and pronounced "lost" (Luke 19:10), "sick" (Isaiah 1:5), "dead" (Ephesians 2:1), and "without hope" (Ephesians 2:12). Man had, by his sins and his lack of response to God's word, judged and condemned himself.

"Not to judge but to save." Compassionate but without compromise; that was Jesus and should be us. But let's be honest, it is a formidable task to find a beginning place, common ground with a culture where ungodliness of every kind is multiplied on every hand. And where, from the world's perspective, Christians are often viewed with suspicion and mistrust. How do we build a bridge that allows us to be the messengers of Jesus who replicate His compassionate care and uncompromising teaching? One answer is found in Acts 17.

Paul finds himself in Athens, Greece, the cradle of democracy and center of philosophy and the arts. He is invited to speak at the Areopagus, a word that referred both to a place and the people who met there. The people were influential, worldly, educated men who would discuss philosophy, current affairs, politics, and religion. To be invited to speak to this audience was an honor and in this fascinating account, Paul shows us ways to find common ground with those whom we have very little in common. But we do have a common problem, namely, sin, and we do have a common solution, namely, Jesus.

What Did Paul Do?

First, He Opened His Eyes

"As I walked around and looked carefully..." (Acts 17:23). And, too, he went to the synagogue and the marketplace (Acts 17:17). The point? He didn't interact and spend his time only with Christians. Paul would later write, "Walk in wisdom toward outsiders, making the best use of the time" (Colossians 4:5). He doesn't assume that when we were baptized, we would seek to live in a Christian cocoon. He assumes we will share life with those who don't know God. Thus, it's imperative that we pray "God may open to us a door for the word" (Colossians 4:3). We need to pray for the interaction with a neighbor, the moms at play group, the co-worker in the next cubicle at work, the teacher in the next classroom or the friend at school or college. We need to pray for an opportunity to say something that introduces the subject of God or faith or hope or church or, most importantly, Jesus.

In Athens, Paul looked for signs of spiritual interest and brilliantly used that as a springboard to talk about the one true God (cf. vv. 22–23). When we pay attention to our world and those in our world, we'll find opportunities created by our similar interests and concerns. That's easy to do once we begin to think in those terms.

Second, He Exposed His Heart

"While Paul was waiting for them in Athens, he was greatly distressed to see that the city was full of idols" (Acts 17:16). "Distressed" not because he was in the wrong pew, but because these people were debating philosophy and erecting statues, but their religion was empty and their souls lost. "Distressed," that is, feeling pain because of what he saw. The question is, that neighbor who is so kind, co-worker who is so helpful, fellow student who is so brilliant, family member who is so loved, does it cause us any pain to realize their soul is lost?

And notice v. 21, "Now all the Athenians and the foreigners who lived there would spend their time in nothing except telling or hearing something new." Doesn't that sound like today? The average American has the attention span of the average gnat. We live in a generation that is often bored and seldom captivated. To teach these people would be a formidable task. But the pain in his heart for the state of their souls outweighed the obstacles to teaching truth in challenging circumstances.

Third, Paul Engaged His Mind

Listen to the language, "So he reasoned in the synagogue with the Jews and the devout persons, and in the marketplace with those who happened to be there. Some of the Epicurean and Stoic philosophers also conversed with him. And some said, "What does this babbler wish to say?" (Acts 17:17–18). This was Paul's pattern, he "reasoned" in Athens, in Thessalonica (Acts 17:2), and in Corinth (Acts 18:4). Preaching and teaching is described as persuading people, reasoning with people. It's interesting that Paul doesn't insult them but, instead, begins with where they are and then skillfully moves them to "Jesus and the resurrection" (Acts 17:18). And make no mistake, the resurrection is the lynch pin of Christian faith. We could have had Christianity without Jesus walking on water, turning water to wine or a variety of other miracles but we could not have Christianity without Jesus rising from the dead.

Fourth, Paul Connected His God

In vv. 24–31, he in essence says, "Let me tell you about the God you don't know."

God created us, (vv. 24a–b)
And while the Athenians needed to know that truth, we need to know it as well. Every person we meet is made in the image of God and should be treated accordingly. That's essential if we're to be effective messengers. Every soul is precious and redeemable. You might well be the bridge that someone needs to find the Lord.

God wants to be close to us, (vv. 27–28)
It's interesting that Paul quotes literature with which they would be familiar and then makes an application to the true God who is our true Father.

God will hold us accountable, (vv. 29–30)
That was, no doubt, not a popular statement but it was a true statement. It was a living example of Jesus' teaching that "you shall know the truth and the truth shall make you free" (John 8:32). He could have just as easily said, "You shall know the truth, but the truth will be hard to hear, may make you miserable, and will be painful to put into practice" and all of that would have been true about the Athenians. But thankfully, some wanted to be truly "free."

Conclusion

And that brings us to a conclusion that is timeless. The preaching of the gospel will forever evoke one of three responses.

Some will reject.
Now when they heard of the resurrection of the dead, some mocked" (Acts 17:32). Some will reject, but not all. It's critically important to remember that truth. If Paul could find interested people in Athens, in the shadow of the Parthenon, then we can find interested people in the U.S. It is our responsibility to introduce people to Jesus. What they decide to do with

Jesus after the introduction is entirely up to them. Thankfully, some will be receptive.

Some will want to hear more.
"Others said, We will hear you again about this" (Acts 17:32). That was terrific news. It meant that there would be ongoing dialogue and continued study. It meant there would be hope.

Some will believe.
"Some men joined him and believed" (Acts 17:34). The question is whether we will be of that ilk. The message is still the same, "Jesus and the resurrection." What will we do with that message? Will we, by faith, plug into the power of God's forgiveness and presence in our lives? And then, will we help others find that power source as well?

Addendum

Peter Wilson was a beloved preacher from the Northwest. He was an early mentor of mine who influenced my life in profound ways. Pete was fond of saying, "The world is lost. The gospel is the power to save. If we don't connect the two, it won't be done." For twenty centuries the challenge has been the same. It is articulated below in a powerful article by Restoration preacher, Benjamin Franklin, in 1856.

> A little preaching on the Lord's day will not do the work. The word should be preached every day and every night, as far as possible. We cannot confine our labors to cities, towns and villages, expecting preaching to be brought to us, as work to a tailor, hatter or shoemaker; but we must go out into the country, among the people, and be among the people, and be one of them, as messengers sent from Heaven to take them to God. We are not to confine ourselves to the fine meeting-house, but, when we can do no better, go to the court-house, the town or city hall, the old seminary, the school-house, or the private dwelling, and preach to the people. We must not wait for the large assembly, but preach to the few, the small, humble and unpromising congregation; we must not merely pretend

to preach, while we are only complaining of them, telling how bad they are; whining over them, and murmuring—showing contempt to them and all their arrangements—but preach to them in the name of the Lord, remembering that in every human form you see, there is a living spirit, upon which Jesus looked when He died and which is worth more than the great globe on which He walked. No matter how lowly, how humble, how poor and uncomely all their temporal arrangements, you will find on acquaintance, some who love the Lord, turn from their sins, and become jewels in the Lord's crown of rejoicing. Do not go into the work with a can't upon your lips, with disheartening words, but preach to them as for life; plead with them with their real danger spread out before your eyes, remembering the reward of him who shall save a soul from death.[1]

DON TRUEX is a native of California but after 27 years in Temple Terrace, FL, he is a Floridian through and through. He and Vickie have two children, Josh & Heather, and two grandchildren, Jocelyn & Kellen. Florida College and Indiana University are his alma maters. Hoosiers, Dodgers, Lakers, Lightning and Bucs are his passions. He has been privileged, truly blessed to preach in several countries and countless states, but loves being with his church family in Temple Terrace more than anything.

1 *American Christian Review,* February, 1856.

CPSIA information can be obtained
at www.ICGtesting.com
Printed in the USA
LVHW050420250821
696017LV00001B/4